SAN
FRANCISCO
STAGES

SAN

FRANCISCO

STAGES

A Concise History,
1849-1986

by

Dean Goodman

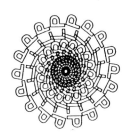

Micro Pro Litera Press
San Francisco

San Francisco Stages: A Concise History, 1849-1986

We would like to thank Adrian Wilson for use of the graphics on the title page, taken from his program for The Interplayers' 1957 production of *Hamlet*.

Assistance in graphics design has been provided by Scott Martin (cover) and Matthew McQueen (title page and cover).

ISBN 0-939477-00-9 (hardcover) and 0-939477-01-7 (softcover)

Library of Congress Catalog Card Number 86-062236

Includes index

This book is dedicated,

with affection and respect,

to the thousands of actors,

stage managers, directors,

writers, designers and technicians

who established the roots of

San Francisco theatre

as it exists today.

Colophon

The text of this book was typeset from the author's typescript on an Apple Macintosh™ computer with a LaserWriter Plus laser printer. The type style is Times™ from the Allied Corporation. The book is printed by Braun-Brumfield, Inc., book manufacturers of Ann Arbor, Michigan, on a 70-lb. coated white stock with a matte finish. The first printing appeared in simultaneous hardcover and softcover editions.

INTRODUCTION

Dean Goodman, actor, director, writer and critic, has been a practitioner of theatre in the Bay Area for over thirty years. In this very informative book he has traced the history of theatre in this region in vivid, compelling detail. He has revealed not only the role of theatre in relation to the San Francisco audience, but has provided delightful insight into the careers and creative thoughts of the many fine artists working here. By taking us inside the very lives of these artists, Mr. Goodman has shed a fascinating light on the noble pro - fession and on San Francisco's reputation as a "great theatre town."

I found the text enormously readable and clear. Mr. Good - man's ideas are solid, coherent and beautifully expressed. This vol - ume will surely establish itself as a major reference that will prove informative and helpful for both playgoers and theatre artists throughout the country.

William Ball
Founding Director
American Conservatory Theatre

PREFACE

In early 1981 Chronicle Books, a division of the Chronicle Publishing Company, gave me a contract and an advance to write a book about Bay area theatre. The publishers and I did not quite see eye to eye on the kind of book we wanted, however. They wanted a tourist guide, with a list of names, addresses and telephone num - bers; I preferred to write a brief history of Bay area theatre as an art and a business, with an analysis of its current state and an educated guess as to where it might be headed in the future. We compro - mised. I delivered a draft of a manuscript much along the lines they wanted. An editor started to work on the text, suggesting cuts and revisions.

In mid-year Chronicle Books ran into some trouble. All copies of a book the company had published on remodeling Victorian houses had to be recalled because it was discovered that the author had plagiarized certain materials. The publishers and the writer now faced the possibility of a suit. Additionally, radio critic Jack Brooks had just brought out his book *Front Row Center*, which was indeed a tourist guide to theatre in the Bay area. The publishers decided that marketing my book at that time presented too many problems for them. They were good enough to let me keep the advance they had paid me, but they returned my manuscript with a letter to the effect that all rights to the material were mine again. I was free to seek an - other publisher.

The major national publishers, and the literary agents with whom I talked, all agreed that the kind of book I wanted to write was important and would contain material which needed to be recorded. While Herbert Blau had written a book abut the founding of the **Actor's Workshop** (*The Impossible Theatre: A Manifesto*, Macmillan, 1964) and John R. Wilk was preparing his manuscript about the early days of the **American Conservatory Theatre** (*The Creation of an Ensemble*, finally published by the Southern Illinois University Press, 1986) no book had been published about the overall San Francisco theatre scene since 1950 (*The San Francisco Stage: A History*, Columbia University Press). But unfortunately, the agents and publishers told me sadly, my kind of book would probably be strictly of regional interest and would therefore have a limited sale. With typesetting, printing and distribution costs being what they are today, no major firm could take the risk, they said. I didn't agree that the book would be of interest only to people in the Bay area; I thought many readers throughout the country would be interested. Still, I was unable to convince anybody of this, and the manuscript remained on a shelf in my closet.

Eventually, William Severson and Harry Bernstein, who were starting a small publishing firm to be called Micro Pro Litera Press, contacted me. They had heard of my book and thought it might be the kind of prestige item which they would like to sponsor. After a few meetings we signed a contract.

San Francisco Stages is not the book which I wrote for Chronicle Books. It was necessary for me to revise and rewrite the entire volume. True, some of the factual material remains the same (after all, one can't alter history!) and some of the same interview quotes appear here as in my original text, but whole sections have been eliminated from the manuscript which I delivered to the Chronicle publishers in 1981. This is no longer a book about the entire Bay area theatre; its contents have been geographically limited to San Francisco. Moreover, a much larger portion of this book deals with theatre history and anecdotes concerning famous players who have performed here. The section about **Equity** waiver houses and the development of small professional theatres is entirely new, as are details concerning productions which have played here over the past few years. Although we would like this book to aid tourists in deciding which theatre companies to patronize when they visit the city of the Golden Gate, and we hope it will be a help to drama students and professional people from other parts of the country who contemplate coming here to live and work, *San Francisco Stages* is not essentially a tourist guide. It is a narrative which attempts to present an accurate, if brief, account of how San Fran - cisco theatre has grown and fluctuated over the past one hundred and thirty-seven years. Obviously, too, many photos are included in this volume which would not have appeared in the previous book.

A comprehensive history of San Francisco theatre, of course, would require several volumes. A process of selection has been necessary in preparing this slender account. If individuals or pro - ducing companies feel offended that their names haven't been men - tioned or photos of their productions haven't been included, I can only apologize. No slight has been intended. As every big touring musical which has played the **Orpheum** or the **Golden Gate** theatre hasn't been mentioned, neither has every avant-garde piece presented in a warehouse south of Market. I must say, however, that information about some companies which I would have liked to include has been omitted because the company agent did not respond to my requests, either for data or for photographs. I have assembled here the best material and the most representative photographs pos - sible, considering the space allowed.

Opera, symphony, ballet, special concerts and cabaret pre - sentations are all parts of the performing arts spectrum, but I have not dealt with them in this volume because they deserve special attention of their own. A few cabaret shows have been mentioned in the narrative because they have been in the nature of intimate revues, with theatrical themes or story lines.

I should point out, too, that it has not been my intent to be overly judgmental concerning the artistic quality and the relative merits of independent productions or producing groups currently operating in San Francisco. That purpose would require a great deal of space to be accomplished properly and in depth; it might be best served in another type of book altogether. I have, however, quoted opinions of experienced people concerning the present theatrical climate in San Francisco, and I have occasionally offered my own opinions and comments when they seemed pertinent.

Perhaps the most controversial aspect of this narrative will be the various remarks about the kind of theatrical criticism which we now have in San Francisco. It has not been my aim to attack any critics on a personal level, but it has indeed been my aim to emphasize that critics do not possess special insights but are as humanly fallible as you and I, and that perhaps their influence on our theatrical climate is not always for the best. In any case, no critic should take offense at what I or anyone else has said here; per - formers themselves suffer far more from critics' barbs than any members of the fourth estate are likely to suffer from the relatively mild observations made about them in *San Francisco Stages.*

Doing the research for this volume has been a fascinating adventure. Over the past several years I have interviewed and talked with hundreds of people who have been eager to tell their stories and to give me their views on the state of theatre in San Francisco, from 1930 to the present day. I can't possibly thank them individually in these pages, so I will thank them collectively. Without their gener - ous help it would not have been possible to prepare this manuscript nor to reproduce the significant photos which the publishers have allowed me to use with the text.

Stage and film star John Barrymore once said that having to refer repeatedly to footnotes or an appendix while one was reading a good book was a little like having to answer the telephone repeatedly while on one's honeymoon. For this reason, I have given bits of side information and credited quotes within text of the narrative; the reader does not have to refer to the back of the book or the bottom of the page for incidental details. I wouldn't want to spoil any love affairs with San Francisco theatre.

Dean Goodman

San Francisco, California
April 15, 1986

vi

CONTENTS

A report on the beginnings of modern theatre in San Francisco, from 1849 to 1966, including data on early plays and players plus information on such companies as the Wayfarers, the Interplayers, the Playhouse, the Actor's Workshop and others.

With the coming of the American Conservatory Theatre in 1967 the city welcomed the most prestigious, artistically and financially suc - cessful company it has ever known.

The San Francisco Civic Light Opera closes its doors, but Carole Shorenstein brings touring musicals to the city in a Best of Broad - way series which is highly successful.

What is a "waiver" theatre and a "waiver" production? Origin of this plan and its development by the Bay Area Advisory Committee for Actors' Equity. Information about the small professional theatres, such as the Eureka, the Magic, the One Act, and the San Francisco Repertory, which have grown out of the waiver plan.

ILLUSTRATIONS

following page 16:

Lotta Crabtree
Maurice Barrymore
Edwin Booth
Playbill for Ethel Barrymore (1907)
The Geary Theatre, circa 1910
Madame Sarah Bernhardt and Lou Telligan performing at San Quentin
Playbill for Cyril Maude starring in *Grumpy* at the Columbia Theatre, 1913
Ina Claire and Douglas Fairbanks, Sr. (1915)
Playbill for Maude Adams and Otis Skinner (1932)
Playbill for Joe E. Brown (1932)
Ina Claire in *The Fatal Weakness*

following page 44:

Jules Irving and Herbert Blau, co-directors of the Actor's Workshop
Priscilla Pointer and Karen Kondazian in a scene from the Actor's Workshop's
     The Crucible, 1955-'56
A scene from the Actor's Workshop's *The Crucible* featuring Jules Irving
Director Loren Gage and Joyce Lancaster in rehearsal of an Interplayers produc-
     tion of *The Madwoman of Chaillot*, 1954
Viveca Lindfors and Joseph Miksak in *Miss Julie* for the Actor's Workshop
Dianne Goldman (later Feinstein) and Dean Goodman in *The Master Builder*,
     1959
Program copy from the Actor's Workshop production of *The Alchemist*, 1960,
     lists names of artists who have had enduring careers
Performers in a May Festival at The Playhouse in 1963 standing in the ruins of
     the Alcazar Theatre on O'Farrell Street
Winifred Mann and Tennessee Williams at rehearsal of an Actor's Workshop
     production of *The Milk Train Doesn't Stop Here Anymore*, 1966

following page 86:

William Ball, founder and original director of A.C.T.
Michael Learned and Paul Shenar starred in A.C.T.'s *Private Lives*, 1971-'72
Fredi Olster and Marc Singer in William Ball's A.C.T. production of *The
     Taming of the Shrew*, 1973-'74
Marsha Mason and Peter Donat in A.C.T.'s *A Doll's House*, 1972-'73
Cast of A.C.T.'s production of Albee's *Tiny Alice* directed by William Ball,
     1975-'76
A 1981 portrait of the San Francisco Mime Troupe
The Lamplighters' *H.M.S. Pinafore* with Eric Morris and Laurel Rice, 1980-'81
Richard Burton in *Camelot* at the Golden Gate Theatre, 1980-'81 season

Nancy Bleiweiss, star of the original *Beach Blanket Babylon*
Angela Lansbury, star of *Sweeney Todd*, 1981
Cast of *Special Friends*, 1981
Liza Feldman and Juliet Mills in *Wait until Dark* at the Alcazar, 1979
Lynn Eldredge, Richard Roemer and Scott Rankine, cast of *Champagne . . . in a cardboard cup!*, 1980
Peter Coyote and Linda Hoy in *An Autobiography of a Pearl Diver* at the Magic Theatre, 1978-'79
Lynn Redgrave in *Sister Mary Ignatius Explains It All for You*, 1984
The cast of the Eureka Theatre's *Cloud Nine*, 1983
Chuck La Font and Sigrid Wurschmidt in the Eureka's *Cloud Nine*, 1983
Carlos Kuhn and Thomas-Mark, leading players in Daniel Curzon's *Beer and Rhubarb Pie* at Theatre Rhinoceros, 1980-'81
Alice Thompson and Terry Baum in the Sharpened Spoons' *Dos Lesbos*, 1981
Marga Gomez, Michele Linfante, Reno and Vicki Lewis in *Pizza*, produced by Lilith, 1980

following page 138:

Kenna Hunt, Jack Shearer, Molly Stadum, Gerald Winer and Francia di Mase, featured in Magic Theatre's production of *The Couch*, 1985
Cast of Asian-American Theatre Company's production of *Thirst*, 1985
Cast of the Eureka's production of *Gardenia*, 1986
J. E. Freeman and Saun Ellis appeared in Marsha Norman's *Getting Out* at the Julian Theatre in 1980
J. J. Johnson and Kitty Newman from Nova Theatre's *Sarah and the Sax*, 1986
Cast of *A Raisin in the Sun* by the Lorraine Hansberry Theatre, 1984
Director J. Kevin Hanlon and Daniel Osmon in rehearsal on the set of Theatre Rhinoceros's *The International Stud*, 1981
The women from Arthur Miller's *Playing for Time*, the One Act Theatre, 1985
Jaston Williams and Joe Sears from the original cast of *Greater Tuna*, 1984
Ebbe Roe Smith, Carol McElheney and Jim Haynie from the Magic Theatre's production of Sam Shepard's *True West*, 1979-'80
Cast of *The Homecoming* in a production by the Chamber Theatre, 1986
The Eureka Theatre's 1986 production of *The Cherry Orchard* featured Abigail Van Alyn and Brian Thompson
A.C.T.'s *'Night Mother* with Marrian Walters and Elizabeth Huddle, 1986
Drew Eshelman, Dean Goodman, Peter Jacobs and Wendell J. Grayson in A.C.T.'s *The Passion Cycle*, 1986
Opéra Comique at A.C.T. with William Paterson and Joan Stuart-Morris, 1985
Edward Hastings, General Director A.C.T., 1986

facing page 153, ABOUT THE AUTHOR:

Dean Goodman as Hamlet, on tour throughout Canada in 1953
Meryl Shaw of SF/BAAC presents Dean Goodman with a plaque in recognition of his years of service to Actors' Equity, March, 1986

1

ROOTS OF GLORY

As young people often find it difficult to imagine that their parents and grandparents ever slept together, so are many of today's playgoers blissfully unaware that thriving theatrical activity existed in San Francisco long before they themselves arrived on the scene. The hustle and bustle of dramatic and musical production which exists throughout the Bay area today did not happen by accident. The diversity of experimental and conventional repertory companies, and the richness of talent which currently abounds in this section of the country can be traced to specific sources.

To gain some perspective of our modern theatre and to acquire a sense of its place in the flow of Time, and also to make educated guesses as to where it might be headed in the future, it is important to examine that theatre's beginnings. Such an endeavor is both an enlightening and a pleasurable experience.

An old schoolhouse in Portsmouth Square was the site of the first recorded theatrical event in San Francisco. This event took place on June 22, 1849, and the evening's program consisted of a series of songs and recitations by one Stephen Massett. We're told that Massett's audience was entirely male. Not many women lived here in those days.

According to Russell Hartley, the founder and initial director of the **Archives for the Performing Arts**, the first recorded theat - rical event in all of California had occurred two years earlier, in the summer of 1847 in Sonoma. This program included a dance, a drama called *The Golden Farmer*, a comic song, and a farce entitled *The Omnibus*.

Prior to that time, theatrical activity throughout the state, in - cluding San Francisco, was limited to fiestas offered by rich Span - ish landowners, religious pageants staged at **Mission Dolores**, and rare performances by vagabond troupes and individual artists.

The first independent local producer of any note was a man named Thomas Maguire, who arrived in San Francisco from New York in 1849. This business-wise gentleman took a quick look around, assessed his opportunities, and set to work. His first move was to buy **Parker House**, on Kearny Street opposite Portsmouth Square, and remodel it into one of the most luxurious gambling pal - aces in the city. But, as Russell Hartley states in an article he wrote for the premier issue of the now defunct **San Francisco Theatre** magazine, Maguire was a man who loved his plays and players. He wanted something more than just a gambling establishment. Conse - quently, he renovated the second story of **Parker House** in magni - ficent style, creating San Francisco's first genuine playhouse, the **Jenny Lind**, in honor of the noted singer, where the most flam - boyant entertainments of the day were soon to be staged. "Inci - dentally," Hartley adds, "the famed Swedish soprano never visited San Francisco."

Six major fires nearly wiped out San Francisco over a two year period, between 1849 and 1851. Maguire's first **Jenny Lind The - atre** was destroyed and so was his second. Maguire was a man not easily defeated, however. He opened a third **Jenny Lind Theatre** on October 8, 1851, an impressive building which later served for a period as the San Francisco **City Hall**. (Clearly, those early San Franciscans had the real pioneer spirit!)

All of Edwin Booth's biographers detail his early days in Cali - fornia. Eleanor Ruggles in her admirably researched book, *Prince of Players* (Norton, 1953) credits *The Mad Booths of Mary - land* (Bobbs-Merrill, 1940) and *Edwin Booth in Old California Days* (The Green Book Album, June, 1911) for information con -

cerning the experiences of Junius Brutus Booth and his sons Junius, Jr. and Edwin when they first arrived in San Francisco.

The young Junius Booth had been hired by Thomas Maguire to manage the **Jenny Lind Theatre**, and on a trip home to the East he extolled the virtues of the land of gold beyond the Sierras to his family. It was four years earlier that the great rush had begun, but fortune hunters still headed westward. In Junius's opinion, how - ever, there were easier ways to make money than by panning gold out of the river beds. The young man told his father, Junius Brutus, about how the miners were exchanging their gold dust for expensive French wines, Cuban cigars, and Dickens' novels in paperback editions. The miners loved a good show, too, said Junius, and they hurried down from their mining camps to see plays and players whenever they had the opportunity.

Junius offered his father an engagement at the **Jenny Lind**. If the whole world was heading west, why not the elder Booth, too?

Junius, Sr. was not so much attracted to the idea of gold, but, getting on in years, he recognized a chance for a last great adven - ture. In the spring of 1852 he scooped up another of his sons, Ed - win, who was playing in stock in Baltimore, and together with Junius, Jr. and the latter's lady friend, a pretty young actress from Boston named Harriet Mace, he headed for California. Edwin was just eighteen.

They entered the Golden Gate and the harbor of San Francisco on July 28, 1852. On Telegraph Hill the black wooden "arm" was raised to signal their arrival. The Long Wharf was crowded with ac - tors who had come to greet them. Maguire had provided a brass band for the occasion, and the enthusiasm of this welcome was a prologue to the illustrious careers which the Booths, particularly Ed - win, were to enjoy in California.

The engagement was only for two weeks, starring Junius Bru - tus with Junius, Jr. and Edwin in support. Maguire had at that time, meaning to build another playhouse, sold the **Jenny Lind** to the city for a town hall. So it was necessary for Junius, Jr., the man - ager, to book his father and brother into Sacramento, where they did not do well. Disappointed, the elder Booth left California, scarcely two months after his auspicious arrival. Edwin stayed on. In No - vember of that year Junius Brutus died. A letter from their mother advised the two sons not to come home and to remain in California.

3

Maguire soon had a new theatre in operation, **San Francisco Hall**. Junius was again Maguire's manager and again he engaged his brother as an actor. Now Edwin began to win his real reputation. A man who saw him at that time sitting on the prompt table, swing - ing his feet, in the middle of **San Francisco Hall** described him "wearing a tattered hat, short monkey jacket, and burst out shoes. He was broke, but gay as a grig and ready to try anything."

He did. He played comedies of manners like *The Critic* and *She Stoops to Conquer*, operettas and farces and rowdy burlesques —the whole gamut. Although still only nineteen he played Richard III and made his first appearance as Hamlet on April 25, 1853.

"Highly creditable," said the *Daily Alta Californian* of his per - formance. "We can even predict a high degree of success for the promising young artist when he shall overcome a few disagreeable faults in intonation and delivery, and reaches a profound conception of the part."

Opposite Catherine Sinclair, the former wife of famed actor Edwin Forrest, young Booth played Petruchio to her Katherine in what was termed Garrick's "mutilated" version of *The Taming of the Shrew*. In May, 1853 he played Benedick, Romeo and Shylock, and apparently this heady succession of great roles in so short a time (and for one so young) was more than he could handle. He was advised by the critics to study his parts better. Junius, afraid his brother was getting a swelled head, jerked him back into a regime of low comedy.

Now Catherine Sinclair, who had leased a grand new theatre, the **Metropolitan**, engaged Edwin for juvenile leads. Soon he played opposite Laura Keene—the same Laura Keene, interestingly and ironically, who later appeared with Edwin's brother John Wilkes at **Ford's Theatre** in *Our American Cousin* on the night that Lincoln was shot. Edwin and Laura Keene did not get along too well as a romantic duo onstage (in fact, Laura Keene was furious with him for ruining her own performance, she said, with his "bad acting") but they did subsequently agree to go on an Australian tour as members of the same company. This tour was a financial disaster and Edwin arrived back in San Francisco in April, 1855 with about ten dollars in his pocket.

Again Catherine Sinclair came to the young actor's rescue. She hired him once more to work for her at the **Metropolitan**, but unfortunately she had lost so much money that she soon had to give

4

up that theatre. Booth drifted a bit and soon found himself billeted in Sacramento.

At this time he was drinking hard. Reviewers chided him for taking his career too casually. (It is a curious thing, but despite his talent and success, Booth was never a truly dedicated actor and was often quite sloppy about details of his performances.) "If he will but apply himself!" the critics cried. "If he will but apply himself indus - triously, unceasingly and perserveringly in his profession, he will ere long rank among the foremost of living actors."

He got a job in Sacramento, but was fired after a month for drinking. Catherine Sinclair, almost like the *good* penny that always turns up, appeared again, rented a small theatre on a back street and re-engaged Edwin. *The Democratic State Journal* reviewed a per - formance of his Richard III in which he forgot his lines not once but repeatedly: "It was palpable that the part had not been studied with the deep concern which an actor of so much promise as Mr. Booth owes not only to an audience but also to himself."

Persuaded finally that he must return east to make his real name, Booth played a benefit performance at the **Metropolitan** in San Francisco, portraying Lear for the first time. Two days later, on September 5, 1856 he said good-bye to California and sailed from the Long Wharf bound for Panama and, eventually, the East Coast. This time he had about five hundred dollars in his pocket.

It was another two decades before Booth returned to San Francisco, twenty years during which he had achieved great acclaim in the East and had become recognized as America's greatest actor. He noticed, of course, many changes in the city. Here for an eight week engagement at the **California**, he smashed all records for the stage in the United States and received tremendous ovations every night. (A young lad named David Belasco was a supernumerary in this company and managed to "walk on" in every play which Booth performed.) Hundreds of people were turned away at the theatre before each performance, and Booth went back to the East in No - vember, 1876, fifty thousand dollars richer.

In 1887 when the great actor came to San Francisco on another tour, he found his room at the **Palace Hotel** filled with pink, white and red camellias. This engagement looked promising, but critics were beginning to carp at Booth for continuing to play Hamlet with his own gray hair.

5

"Hamlet!" he scoffed. "A wig for Hamlet? If they don't like my Hamlet—let them stay away!"

But, with some sadness, he capitulated to his advisors. He wore a wig.

Booth concluded this engagement with a single performance as the Moor in *Othello*. By today's standards, he was far from an old man yet, but he had dissipated a great deal and his health was not too good. He was feeling dizzy at times, and he missed his daughter Edwina.

Although Edwin Booth appeared twice again in San Francisco during the next three years, business was not as spectacular as it had been for him in the past, and after 1890 he made no more trips to the West. The man whom some people still consider the greatest actor America has ever produced died in New York on June 7, 1893. He was fifty-nine years of age. It was said that he looked as if he were in his seventies.

At about the same time Booth started to make his mark in California—in May of 1853, to be exact—the colorful and rather notorious Lola Montez made her debut in San Francisco. A number of theatres rivaling Maguire's were now springing up, and Montez opened a highly successful season of dance and drama at the **American Theatre**, located on Sansome Street between California and Sacramento. Following each evening's performance as Lady Teazle in *School for Scandal* , the actress offered as the pièce de ré - sistance her sensational "Spider Dance," which immediately took the city by storm and was the talk of the town.

Dance was very popular in those days and between 1852-'55 three major European ballet troupes played in San Francisco. The famous **Christy's Minstrels** settled here in 1854, later combined with **Maguire's Minstrels**, and became known as the **San Francisco Minstrels**. The minstrel show, a sort of predecessor of vaudeville, was by far the most popular form of entertainment in the West at that time.

Lotta Crabtree, who had her beginnings in Grass Valley as a protégée of Lola Montez, made her San Francisco debut in 1859 at the **Red Opera House**, and went on to become one of the shining lights of the American stage. Lotta's Fountain, her gift to the city, still stands at the Market Street intersection of Geary and Kearny Streets.

6

The first transcontinental railroad was completed in 1869 and it then became possible to move entire troupes and carloads of elab - orate sceneries from the East to the West in a matter of days. All of the great stars, from Europe as well as the eastern states of America, now extended their tours to this area. The touring show became, as it remains today, a staple item of San Francisco's theatrical activity.

The great theatres of those years were **Wade's Opera House**, which became the **Grand Opera House**, the **Baldwin Theatre**, and the **California Theatre**. The **California** and **Baldwin** devoted themselves to major attractions from the East, while the **Grand Opera House** offered entertainment more local in origin, from opera to acrobats.

It was in the spring of 1882 that Oscar Wilde visited San Fran - cisco on his famous lecture tour across country. "I have nothing to declare except my genius," announced Oscar when his boat docked in New York.

Wilde's reputation as an aesthete had preceded him, and Americans regarded him as something of a buffoon and came to hear him speak more out of curiosity than anything else. He had yet to write his most famous plays, and in 1882 he was merely sharpening the wit for which he later became both famous and infamous. (In fact, it's claimed by some that Wilde was trained in the well-turned epigram by his mentor, artist James McNeill Whistler, something of a dandy himself and no slouch when it came to verbal repartee. One story has it that when, at some gathering or other, Whistler made a particularly delicious remark, Wilde laughed heartily, "Oh, I wish I'd said that!" To which Whistler replied dryly, "You will, Oscar. You will.")

In his book *Oscar Wilde* (Viking Press, 1973) Martin Fido points out that as a lecturer, wild Oscar left something to be desired. His manner on the speaker's platform was poor. "His well-modulated tenor voice, which in later years would become rich and plummy, lacked the full resonance to which American audiences were accustomed." He read his words directly from a script in front of him, he was not considered terribly funny, and some of his audiences were bored.

Despite this, his tour was a success. Women, particularly, took to him, both on the stage and on a social level. During his lifetime Wilde made friends with scores of prominent women who were devoted to him—Sarah Bernhardt, Helena Modjeska, Lily Langtry,

Ellen Terry, and even our own Harriet Beecher Stowe!—though none of them were able to give him much help when he later got into serious trouble.) His costume on tour (knee breeches, patent leather pumps, voluminous cape, flowing tie, yellow gloves, topped by a romantic hat covering his long hair) was part of a well-planned publicity stunt. This publicity attracted people to hear him speak, but his lectures were essentially quite serious and intelligent listeners came to realize that here was a man who should be taken seriously.

His reception in San Francisco exceeded anything he had yet experienced in the States, according to Fido. Fashionable audiences attended his lectures at **Platt Hall**, and he did manage to toss off an amusing comment or two. In favorably comparing a Chinese laborer's teacup with the dinnerware in luxury hotels, for example, he anticipated a tone which his own creation, Lady Bracknell, might have employed in *The Importance of Being Earnest*: "We do not want a soup-plate whose bottom seems to vanish in the distance. One feels neither safe nor comfortable under such conditions."

The audience at his first **Platt Hall** lecture applauded him when he suggested that "the value of the telephone is the value of what two people have to say."

Oscar Wilde, like so many others before and since, fell in love with San Francisco. He declared that the city "possessed all the attractions of the next world"—which sums up, as briefly and succinctly as anyone could, the fascination that this Baghdad-by-the-Bay has always held for artists, businessmen, and people from all walks of life.

Both Maurice Barrymore and Georgie Drew Barrymore, the parents of John, Ethel and Lionel, were among the front rank players who came to the West and included San Francisco in their itineraries after the transcontinental railroad came into use. It took seven days to travel by rail from New York to San Francisco in 1875, says James Kotsilibas-Davis in *Great Times, Good Times* (Doubleday, 1977) and Maurice, a romantic juvenile, first played here in a company managed by the Broadway producer Augustin Daly. Eight years later, married to Georgie and now a father, Maurice (or Barry, as his intimates called him) by this time also playwright, leading man and sometime lover to the hypnotic Polish actress Helena Modjeska was back here with his wife, family and mistress, appearing in a repertoire which included *A Midsummer*

Night's Dream, Adrienne Lecouvreur, As You Like It, Twelfth Night and *Mary Stuart*.

In the summer, a couple of years later, one of Barrymore's own plays, starring Modjeska (who was later to make her home in California) and titled *Nadjezda* opened in San Francisco at the **Baldwin Theatre**. "Although *Nadjezda* is full of strong dramatic situations, cleverly handled," said the San Francisco *Bulletin* in reviewing the production, "it is too bloody in its motif to inspire enthusiasm."

The bill was changed very shortly. The *Bulletin* was luke - warm about Barry's performance opposite Modjeska in *Camille*. "Maurice Barrymore was a good Armand," wrote the critic, "and that is about all that can be said about him." (Well, that's about all critics have been able to say about any Armand, since Marguerite Gautier is the primary and prize role in *La Dame aux camélias*, and all any actor who plays Armand is required to do is stand around and look handsome and adoring.) But Barry's work in *As You Like It* evoked a little more enthusiasm. "Mr. Barrymore infuses a good deal of life and vigor into the part of Orlando," conceded the *Bulletin*.

Georgie Drew Barrymore did not always appear with her husband. As they continued their on-again, off-again marriage (and as she alternately ignored her husband's philandering or berated him for it) Georgie accepted many engagements which separated her from Barry. She was particularly popular in San Francisco. In a play called *The Sportsman* "she was a decided hit," reported the *Chronicle* in 1892, "playing with a spirit, a life and a breeziness and a perfection of farce acting which brought the curtain down upon an outburst of applause."

While in the Bay area with that engagement Georgie was offered a large sum by L. R. Stockwell, manager of the **Stockwell Theatre**, to star in a series of special matinees which would not interfere with her regular performances. She wanted to accept the offer, but her contract with Charles Frohman forbade outside en - gagements. She telegraphed him in New York to ask his permission to do the matinees. "Will you release me?" Frohman's reply was to the point: "No." She wired back: "Oh."

During this time Georgie was troubled with a bronchial congestion. A year later, in 1893, when she was playing in Santa Barbara, L. R. Stockwell traveled from San Francisco to see her and to offer her an autumn engagement in his theatre. She was able to accept him this time. But her congestion was growing worse. She died on July 12. "It was only then that we knew she had consump - tion," said daughter Ethel, who was with her mother at the time of her death.

In general, though occasionally rapped in the press, audiences and critics liked Maurice Barrymore and they noticed an increasing depth to his acting after Georgie's death. Though numbed by her passing he married again only a year later, in 1894, and continued with his career. In 1895 he was back at the **Columbia** in San Francisco, starring in repertory and concluding his engagement triumphantly as Lord Illingworth in the first local production of Oscar Wilde's *A Woman of No Importance*.

Hospitalized, heavily sedated, his mind almost gone, Maurice Barrymore died at Amityville in the spring of 1905.

Son Lionel was due to go on the road, for the first time as a star, in *The Other Girl*. He visited his father in the hospital, shortly before the elder man's death.

"Where did you say you were going?" asked Barry.

"West, and then to San Francisco."

"You're a God-damned liar, Lionel," his father snorted. "Everyone knows that San Francisco has been destroyed by earth - quake and fire."

Maurice Barrymore uttered those words, almost as an eerie prophecy, a solid year before San Francisco was indeed destroyed by earthquake and fire. Lionel wasn't present on that fateful April morning. John Barrymore, however, was in the city.

Gene Fowler, in his book *Good Night, Sweet Prince* (The Blackstone Company, 1944) mentions that John Barrymore, the matinee idol son of Maurice and brother of Lionel, was in San Francisco at the time of the great quake. At first Barrymore was reported among the missing. He wanted to assure his family of his safety, but with telegraph services lacking and personal messages banned, he could only manage to tag a short message onto the end of a news bulletin to New York. The message was to his sister Ethel and he told how he had been thrown out of bed by the tremblor and had wandered dazedly into the street. An Army sergeant had thrust a shovel into his hand and made him work for twenty-four hours among the ruins of the city.

10

Ethel read this message to their uncle John Drew and asked if he believed it. "Every word," replied Uncle Jack. "It took an act of God to get him out of bed, and the United States Army to put him to work."

The beautiful Maxine Elliott was not born in the Bay area, but she was the very next thing to a native daughter. Her life began in Rockland, Maine shortly after the Civil War. (The exact date of her birth is a little hazy, because like many actresses she tried to mix people up concerning her age and gave different birthdates to the press.) Married young to a man who was something of a drunkard, she fled her husband's bed and board and, not quite twenty-one, came west to live with her father and his new bride who had bought a home in Oakland.

Maxine Elliott had no passionate love of acting or the theatre, but everybody told her she ought to go on the stage because she was so beautiful. She could be spontaneously amusing in family groups and at small parties, but she had been self-conscious even reciting in school and the thought of becoming a professional actress terrified her. She had to do something with her life, however, after her sepa-ration from her husband, so she decided (after dismissing the alter-natives) to go to New York to seek her fortune in the theatre.

In her book *My Aunt Maxine* (Viking, 1964) Diana Forbes-Robertson quotes Alexander Woollcott as saying that Maxine Elliott could not be considered a bad actress, she was simply a *non*-actress. She became immensely popular and successful, though she rarely received good reviews from the critics. Years later when Lee Shubert tried to persuade her not to retire, after she had saved a tidy little nest-egg, suggesting that she would certainly miss the glamour and excitement of her life in the public eye, she replied, "I'll miss it about as much as the early Christian martyrs missed the man-eating lions in the arena." When in New York in 1933 she told the press, "There's no good talking to me. I never really liked the theatre. I just happened to be in it. Night after night I have played in successes and they became drearier and drearier."

In New York, after she left Oakland as a young woman, Maxine gained some confidence under the tutelage of Dion Boucicault who accepted her as a student. It was he who taught her to take stock of her assets: statuesque beauty, ladylike speech, dig-nity and grace. He also helped her to choose her professional name. (She was born Jessie Dermott.) When Boucicault died and she went

11

job hunting she was so self-assured that she left her first interview with exactly what she had come for. She was engaged as a small part player with an English company that was appearing on Broad - way in repertory. She completed the spring season with that com - pany and was re-engaged to go with the company on a cross-country tour beginning in September, 1891.

Maxine Elliott's first professional appearance in San Francisco was with this company (its star Edward S. Willard is little remem - bered today) on December 14, 1891. In this company were also Blanche Bates (who got better notices than Maxine and became a star herself) and Tyrone Power, the father of the latter day film star. Gertrude Elliott, Maxine's sister, was also a member of this com - pany. Soon the celebrated comedian Nat C. Goodwin arrived in San Francisco with a company, became smitten with Maxine, and wooed her to join him on an Australian tour. Thus began not only a ro - mance which led to a wedding but an acting team which was to be quite prominent in the American theatre for the next several years. It all started in San Francisco.

Maxine Elliott and Nat Goodwin did not marry at once. Maxine had secured her divorce but Goodwin was married to another wo - man when they met. Their affair was the subject of much scandal and they could not wed until two years later, after Goodwin's divorce became final, in 1898. By this time they had returned to the United States from Australia, had co-starred in another play in New York and were on tour. Throughout her career Maxine, like many actresses, was plagued by scandal and had love affairs, or at least rumored love affairs, with such dignitaries as J. Pierpont Morgan and King Edward VII of England. (Her fabulous chateau in France was sometimes leased by the Prince of Wales during his courtship to Wallis Simpson and after their marriage.)

The Goodwins appeared in San Francisco in the spring of 1900 in *When We Were Twenty-One*, their greatest success as an acting couple. When Maxine's sister, Gertrude, married Johnston Forbes-Robertson, acclaimed as the greatest Hamlet since Booth, Maxine was very upset. She had hoped for a "better" marriage for her little sister, to a man in a more respectable walk of life than the theatre, and it was hard for her to realize that Gertrude had found exactly what she was looking for in her new husband.

The Goodwins had a fling at playing Shakespeare—nearly all actors did in those days!—but they were not very successful at it.

The marriage began to flounder. Nat was drinking too much and often humiliated Maxine by public scenes and cheap flirtations with other women. She considered leaving Nat and starring on her own, but they did not officially separate until May, 1903. In San Fran - cisco, Nat Goodwin told the press that their parting was thoroughly amicable. They had difficulty finding scripts with parts suitable for the two of them, they could make more money working separately, etc., etc. Clyde Fitch, in the meantime, had written a new play ex - pressly for Maxine. She opened on Broadway as a full-fledged star in *Her Own Way* on September 28, 1903. The minute she achieved this goal, she began planning for another: her eventual retirement from the stage. "You won't find anything very interesting in the the - atre after saying 'I love you' night after night precisely at 10:28, plus the matinees," she said.

Whether it's true, as gossip had it, that J. P. Morgan built the **Maxine Elliott Theatre** on 39th Street in New York for his mis - tress may never be known. (In her book *My Aunt Maxine*, Diana Forbes-Robertson says that while many actors, including her father Johnston Forbes-Robertson, received more acclaim for their artistry, you couldn't ignore the fact that Maxine was immensely popular, left an estate of a million dollars when she died in 1940, and had had a theatre named after her. Very few players of that era, or this, achieved the same goals.) In any event, the corporate papers for pur - chase of the 39th Street property name only Lee Shubert as party of the first part and Maxine Elliott Goodwin as party of the second part. But the building was constructed and Maxine profited from its lease during many years, until her death. The theatre was used for a time as a broadcasting studio and was finally demolished in 1959.

In 1946 I co-directed a production of Noel Coward's *Tonight at 8:30* for the **Equity Library Theatre** in New York. It was very successful and Broadway producer John Golden moved the show into the **Maxine Elliott Theatre** for some special perfor - mances. The building was getting a bit run-down at the time, but it was still charming and it was a thrill to be working in a theatre which had been built by and for such a legendary lady. The leading woman in *Tonight at 8:30* was Marrian Walters, who was sub - sequently hired by Golden to make her debut on Broadway in *Made in Heaven*, starring Donald Cook. Aficionados of San Francisco theatre will recognize Walters' name immediately. She has been a prominent actress on the local scene for the past twenty years, first

13

in long runs of *Private Lives, Under the Yum-Yum Tree* and other plays at the **Little Fox Theatre** and the **On Broadway**, next with Ben Kapen's **Melodyland** in Berkeley where she appeared with Robert Goulet in *Carousel* and with Leslie Uggams in *The Boy Friend*—we were together again for those two!—and more recently she has been seen in a wide variety of parts with the **American Conservatory Theatre**, scoring great personal successes in Maugham's *The Circle* and in Noel Coward's *Hay Fever*. Those performances at the **Maxine Elliott Theatre** in 1946 were impor-tant at the beginning of Walters' career.

The great Sarah Bernhardt appeared in San Francisco several times, both in vaudeville and on her various "farewell" tours. With a repertoire of no less than a dozen plays the Divine One was here in April of 1891 and then, after a couple of months in Hawaii and Aus-tralia, she was back for another stand in September of the same year. In 1906 she came to play the city when everything was still in smoldering ruins from the great quake and the fire. In *Madame Sarah* (Houghton-Mifflin, 1967) biographer Cornelia Otis Skinner tells how Bernhardt, undaunted by the lack of a place to perform in San Francisco, took her company across the bay and appeared in the Greek open-air theatre at Berkeley. She later volunteered to give a recital for the prisoners at San Quentin. "What the men in black-striped uniforms thought of the strangely exotic-looking woman who acted for them in an incomprehensible language has not been handed down in the annals of San Quentin," concludes Skinner.

Stories are legend about how Bernhardt always demanded her salary in gold coins before each performance. There is a tale about how, riding in a taxi up that perilous hill to the **Fairmont Hotel** during one of her stays in San Francisco, she ordered her man-servant, a mousey little man called Pitou, to close the cab window. Somehow, as Pitou was trying to do this, the door to the cab swung open, and the famous strong box also opened and gold coins were rolling every which way at the corner of California and Powell Streets. A few disappeared beneath the cable car tracks. Sarah screamed, and shopkeepers came forth to help collect the scattered loot from that day's performance.

The quake of April 12, 1906, Russell Hartley's records tell us, destroyed all but one of San Francisco's theatres, **The Chutes**, in the Fillmore District. However, theatres popped up again like mush-rooms—just as they had done during the fires of 1849-'51—and by

14

December, 1906 San Francisco theatrical life was booming once more.

New theatres included the **Van Ness Theatre** at Van Ness and Grove, the **Valencia** and the **Columbus**. During the second decade of the new century the major theatres were the **Columbia** (now the **Geary**), the **Alcazar**, the **Savoy**, and the **Cort**.

Between the years 1909-'13 a French-born artist, Maurice Del Mue, teamed up with writers Waldemar Young and Ralph E. Renaud to do a series of special features for the front page "Dramatic and Society" section of the Sunday *Chronicle*. The men developed a practical and very effective way of working. While the writer interviewed the celebrity, artist Del Mue would make his drawing of the subject. The text of the interview was then arranged tastefully and artistically around the colored drawing on the page. Del Mue mixed his own inks to achieve the unusual shades—brilliant reds, soft mauves and lavenders, rich acid greens and electric blues. Some of these remarkable pages are on file in Hartley's **Archives for the Performing Arts** and have occasionally been displayed under glass at the main branch of the **San Francisco Public Library**.

Billie Burke was the subject of the *Chronicle* interview and Del Mue's drawing on Sunday, October 10, 1909. This charming story, titled "The Morals of the Stage" was written while Burke was here at the **Van Ness Theatre** in a play called *Love Watches*. Burke was not yet Mrs. Florenz Ziegfeld, the flighty comedy char - acter she developed and exhibited in so many M-G-M movies of the 30s was far off, and her classic Glinda the Good in that equally classic film *The Wizard of Oz* was still three decades in the future.

David Belasco, born in San Francisco in 1859, that lad who managed to "walk on" with Booth during every performance when the great actor was here in 1876, carved out a notable career for himself in New York both as playwright and producer and is cred - ited, to a large extent, with introducing realism to the American stage. His *Rose of the Rancho* was at the **Baldwin Theatre** in 1909. In August of that same year, Dustin Farnham (later to achieve fame as a hero in silent films) was at the **Van Ness Theatre** in *Cameo Kirby*, sub-titled "A Brilliant Play of Romance and Love." John Drew was at the **Cort**, appearing with his niece Ethel. Eddie Foy—yes, the same Eddie Foy who was father of the 7 Little Foys!—was playing in *Mr. Hamlet of Broadway* at the **Valencia Theatre** (a structure which, incidentally, still stands as a **Greek**

Orthodox Church). George M. Cohan, with his mother and father and sister, was playing, appropriately enough, "a family show" at the **Van Ness Theatre**. This playhouse was on the corner where we now have the new and beautiful **Louise M. Davies Symphony Hall**.

The renowned Mrs. Fiske was one of the earliest portrayers of Ibsen characters in this country, although *Pillars of Society* seems an odd vehicle for a female star to choose to show her talents, since the leading characters in this Ibsen classic are male. Perhaps Mrs. Fiske considered herself not the type for Nora in *A Doll's House* and *Hedda Gabler* too scandalous a role and play for a lady of her dignity to perform. At any rate, she was presenting herself in *Pillars of Society* at the **Columbia Theatre** in 1910. Shakespearean actor Robert Mantell also played the **Columbia** in repertory and a photograph of the theatre at that time shows his name prominently displayed on a billboard in front of the building.

If the plays performed by leading actors of this era seem to range from the sublime to the ridiculous, it must be remembered that in the early 1900s there was nothing much in-between. We had not yet developed first-rate dramatists in this country; we had no classic playwrights of our own. Eugene O'Neill, Tennessee Williams, Arthur Miller and Lillian Hellman were far ahead. Serious actors, therefore, had to perform the plays of writers who had established prestigious reputations in other countries. Leading stars like Mantell, acting teams like Sothern and Marlowe, and actor-managers like Forbes-Robertson went on the road in Shakespearean repertoire. Lesser artists played frivolous, quickly forgotten farces or light comedies or melodramas which, to our sophisticated tastes today, would seem absurd. In 1910 television and radio were unheard of and even silent films were in their infancy; the theatre was all things to all men. Vaudeville sketches and good rip-snorting melodrama filled the needs which TV sit-coms, variety programs, car-chase and science fiction or horror films satisfy today.

Lillian Russell, never much of an actress or a singer but a beauty with a warm and winning personality, appeared in San Francisco many times. In 1910 she was at the **Columbia Theatre** in *In Search of a Sinner*. How's that for the title of a show starring a lady whose audience appeal was based mainly on her sexual attractions? Otis Skinner, his greatest hit *Kismet* still ahead of him, also played the **Columbia** that same year in *Your Humble Servant*.

16

Lotta Crabtree (Photo: San Francisco Library Archives)

Maurice Barrymore (left) and Edwin Booth (above)
(Photos: San Francisco Library Archives)

Beginning Monday July 8

Matinees Wednesday and Saturday

CHARLES FROHMAN

——— PRESENTS ———

ETHEL BARRYMORE

In the Fantastic Comedy, in Three Acts,

"CAPTAIN JINKS"

by Clyde Fitch

Playbill from 1907
(above; San Francisco
Library Archives)

The Geary Theatre, circa
1910, when it was known
as the Columbia (left)

Madame Sarah Bernhardt, with her leading man Lou Telligan, in a rare pose from *Madame sans gêne*, photographed at San Quentin Prison Camp, February 22, 1913. (above; Photo: San Francisco Library Archives)

While re-plastering and painting the box-office of the Geary Theatre in 1986, workmen found this yellowed playbill (facing page) in the walls of the building. Cyril Maude was an eminent British actor, popular in this country, who played the Geary (then the Columbia Theatre) in *Grumpy* in 1913.

M͟r͟ Cyril Maude

IN HIS INTERNATIONAL TRIUMPH

GRUMPY

A MELODRAMATIC COMEDY IN FOUR ACTS
By HORACE HODGES AND T. WIGNEY PERCYVAL.

COLUMBIA THEATRE
SAN FRANCISCO, CAL.

Two Weeks Com.
MONDAY   APRIL 23

Matinees Wednesday and Saturday

In 1915 when Ina Claire was under contract to Cecil B. De Mille in Hollywood, she posed on the lot with Douglas Fairbanks, Sr. (above).

Two playbills from 1932 (facing page)
(San Francisco Library Archives)

One of Ina Claire's last great Broadway successes was George Kelly's *The Fatal Weak -
ness* in which she appeared in San Francisco at the Geary Theatre in December, 1947.
(Photo: Vandamm Studio, New York)

Ruth St. Denis, who considered San Francisco her second home, appeared here in dance concerts over twenty-five times, long before she partnered with Ted Shawn to create history in the field of dance. Isadora Duncan, whose ambition was to have a child by each of several hand-picked gentlemen throughout the world, was a native daughter of the Bay area. (She wrote to George Bernard Shaw: "Think what a child we could produce, with your brains and my beauty!" To which Shaw replied, "Yes, my dear—but suppose the child turned out to have *your* brains and my beauty?") Luisa Tetrazzini, who was discovered in San Francisco while performing with the **Tivoli Opera Company**, was singing at **Dreamland Auditorium** (subsequently called **Winterland**) in 1910. For years Tetrazzini gave free Christmas concerts at Lotta's Fountain.

Olga Nethersole, billed as "The World's Greatest Emotional Actress" was at the **Savoy Theatre** in *Sister Beatrice and the Enigma* in 1911. Years earlier, Nethersole had seduced Maurice Barrymore into being her leading man after his break with Modjeska—and, considering their reputations, it's likely she seduced him in a couple of other ways, too. Marie Dressler was a great hit here in 1911 in *Tillie's Nightmare*. This was long before she won the Academy Award appearing with Garbo in *Anna Christie* (1930) and even before she made some of her successful silent films. The French soubrette Anna Held was at the **Columbia Theatre** in *Miss Innocence*, supported by a bevy of chorus beauties (**75** *Anna Held Girls* **75**). An article in a December, 1911 issue of the Sunday *Chronicle* titled "What Goes On Behind Anna Held's Eyes?" explored the enigmatic appeal of the winsome and tantalizingly sexy Miss Held. It was in San Francisco that Flo Ziegfeld later built the sunken tub in a home for Anna Held while she was appearing here and where, the press was informed, the actress took daily baths in goats' milk.

In 1912 Ethel Barrymore was enjoying one of her periodic turns on the **Orpheum** vaudeville circuit, which she did several times throughout her career between more important engagements in New York. This time in San Francisco she was playing a one-acter called *The Twelve Pound Look* . Charlotte Greenwood was also on the **Orpheum** circuit in 1912. This tall, lanky comedienne, famous for her sunny personality and her eccentric dancing (which included amazing feats with her long legs) continued her career well into the 1940s, when she supported Betty Grable and Alice Faye in many of

17

their musicals for **Twentieth-Century Fox**. In 1912 she had a partner in her vaudeville act, which was billed as "Burnham and Greenwood—Two Girls and a Piano." The February 25, 1912 edition of the Sunday *Chronicle* carried a provocatively titled article, "The Secret of the Greenwood Kick."

An actor named De Wolf Hopper achieved his greatest success reciting a dramatic poem, "Casey at the Bat," which he once swore he had performed close to 6,000 times. He was also Hedda Hop - per's husband, but since Hedda didn't achieve her prominence as an acerbic Hollywood columnist until De Wolf was long gone from her life, one couldn't say his marriage to the lady was a claim to fame at that time. In 1912 De Wolf Hopper was playing in San Francisco as, of all things, Koko in Gilbert and Sullivan's *The Mikado*. The production was at the **Cort Theatre**.

William Faversham, a romantic stage idol, was also at the **Cort** that year, in a comedy called *The Faun*. Margaret Anglin was in town in *The Green Stockings*. The **Georgia Minstrels** were here, too, featuring McIntyre and Heath, a peculiar pair of perform - ers who conducted an amazing life-time feud and only spoke to each other onstage, with prepared dialogue. Chauncy Olcott, who got his start in San Francisco singing in blackface with **Emerson's Minstrels**, was back in town in 1913 starring in *The Isle O' Dreams* at the **Columbia Theatre**. Elsie Janis, who did so much to entertain the troops overseas during World War I, appeared in two musicals in San Francisco during 1912—*The Slim Princess* and *The Pink Lady*.

Julian Eltinge, who may go down in the history of the Ameri - can stage as one of its most unique performers, was an artist of high calibre. He appeared in drag, but he was not a drag queen. There was nothing "camp" about him and he was much more than just a female impersonator. In essence he was an illusionist, a true male actress. He often played two roles in his productions, coming on first as a dashing and handsome young leading man and then ap - pearing late in the plot as a *femme fatale*. He was in *The Fascinating Widow* at the **Cort Theatre** in San Francisco in 1912.

Charles Taylor, Laurette Taylor's first husband (and whose name she kept throughout her professional career, even after her second marriage to *Peg O' My Heart* author Hartley Manners), was a writer of the kind of melodrama which was immensely popular around the turn of the century. His very first melo was produced at San Francisco's **Bijou Theatre** in 1891. It was called *The Devil's Punch Bowl* and later became one of his greatest successes under the title *Yosemite*. Curiously, Marguerite Courtney who authored a biography of her mother titled *Laurette* (Rinehart and Company, 1955) has done a very good piece of work in detailing the actress's career but she has made little mention of Laurette's appearances in San Francisco. Courtney tells, for example, of Laurette appearing in New York in a not too successful play called *The Girl in Waiting* in 1910, taking it on the road and closing it (supposedly forever) in 1911. But San Francisco's Sunday *Chronicle* of August 18, 1912 features a Del Mue drawing of Laurette, an interview titled "The Different Actress" and indicates that she was appearing at the local **Alcazar Theatre** in *The Girl in Waiting* in 1912. (Laurette Taylor was, indeed, a "different" actress and one of the few whom Stanislavski praised when he visited America with his **Moscow Art Theatre Company** in 1924. Her career went into a decline in the late 20s and 30s when she was suffering from alcoholism, but she made a sensational comeback in Tennessee Williams' *The Glass Menagerie* in 1945. Those of us who were fortunate enough to see her hauntingly beautiful perfor-mance in that production will probably never forget it. It had a strange, vague, delicate, ephemeral quality which words cannot adequately describe.) In any event, though her daughter Marguerite doesn't mention it, Laurette Taylor did appear in San Fran-cisco—and, according to the *Chronicle*, in *The Girl in Waiting* in 1912.

David Warfield, whose greatest success was in a sentimental drama called *The Music Master*, was interviewed in the *Chronicle* on June 23, 1912.

"I love San Francisco with all the love that a man can have for a town," Warfield is quoted as saying. "Why shouldn't I, indeed? I was born here, cradled in the town. Many of my nearest and dearest friends are here. It is home. I have my residence in New York by necessity, but if the choice were mine—if I were able to fix it tomorrow—I would stay here and never want to go away. . . . Always, when the chance offers, I return here for my real rest and my real vacation."

In this brief synopsis of San Francisco theatrical history I have placed emphasis on plays and players of renown or distinction and whose names might have some significance for modern readers, or I have related tales about the period which seem amusing or colorful. While it's true that many actors had their beginnings in the Bay area and then came back as stars, and while it's true that the important Broadway producers and managers sent road companies to San Francisco (as they do even today) it should not be concluded that all of the theatrical activity here involved touring shows. There have always been locally based productions and there have always been actors who, though they may never have achieved international or even national fame, have been popular in the smaller sphere of the Bay area and have been content to make their homes here.

Russell Hartley's records, for example, tell us that the **Alca - zar** was managed until the early 1920s by Belasco and Mayer and run as a resident stock company with local guest players. One of these local stars was Emilie Melville who came to be known, even - tually, as the grand old lady of the San Francisco stage. Miss Mel - ville arrived here in February, 1868, convulsing her audiences as Jenny Leatherlungs in a satire on Jenny Lind. In 1876 she turned to grand opera, singing in *La Traviata* at the **Baldwin**. She went on to become one of the mainstays of the local **Tivoli Opera Asso - ciation**, as well as an accomplished *danseuse*. When her voice began to fail, she became a dramatic actress, one of the best. Notices of her appearances in character parts can be found as late as 1931. She finished her San Francisco career as a dramatics teacher in the city.

Ina Claire, who began as a showgirl and who went on to be - come one of the most skillful players of sophisticated comedy on the American stage, was in San Francisco in 1918 appearing in an early hit, *Polly with a Past*. At the same time Sarah Bernhardt happened to be playing here, doing a turn on the **Orpheum** circuit. Claire was asked if she would like to meet Bernhardt. She said she would be delighted and she was taken backstage by a mutual friend to be introduced to the legendary French actress after one of her perfor - mances.

"This is Ina Claire," said the friend, Donald MacDonald, as he presented her to Bernhardt, "a great American star."

20

"Oh, no, no," said Ina, quickly protesting. "I'm not a great star, really. I'm just an actress who happens to be a bit popular at the moment."

Madame nodded. "Ah," she said. "First come popular. Then come great. The public never make mistake."

Ina Claire married San Francisco attorney William Wallace in 1939. She did a few more plays in New York, but completely retired after T. S. Eliot's *The Confidential Clerk* in the early 50s. (She frequently went on the road with her productions and, in addition to *Polly with a Past*, appeared in San Francisco in Sherwood's *Reunion in Vienna*, which the Lunts had done on Broadway.) After her husband's death Ina Claire, vibrantly alert and attractive, continued to live in San Francisco. It was my privilege, at the **Bay Area Theatre Critics** Awards Show in 1979, to introduce her and to present her with a special trophy in recognition of her many years of outstanding work in the American theatre. She charmed the audience when she looked skeptically at the microphone in front of her. "In my day," she said, "we didn't need *these!*" The great lady has now passed on.

A man named Reginald Travers became an important force in San Francisco theatre when, about 1912, he organized the **Players Club** and presented plays and operettas, chiefly works of Gilbert and Sullivan. Travers went to New York in 1922, where he started the **Cherry Lane Theatre**, but he came back in 1925 and resumed his work with the **Players**. The **Players Club** then became the **Players Guild**, staging plays by Shaw, O'Neill, Molnar and others. In September, 1927, Travers opened another theatre, **The Community**, and his premier production was Noel Coward's *Hay Fever*, starring Douglas Fairbanks and Emilie Melville.

Alfred Lunt played one of his earliest engagements in Berkeley at the **Greek Theatre**. This was in 1915. He was hired by Margaret Anglin, a romantic actress of the period, to serve as her leading man in a repertoire of three Greek tragedies for a six week booking. Lunt was auditioned for the job by Howard Lindsay, who was later to become half of a famous playwriting team with Russell Crouse and who was then Miss Anglin's stage manager. Lindsay thought Lunt was terrible, an evaluation which he later admitted was one of the most colossal misjudgments in the history of the American

21

theatre. But Miss Anglin said, "I think the boy has quality. True, he *is* ugly—but it is a handsome ugliness, rather like the Vanderbilts!" (The men of the wealthy Vanderbilt family had large faces with bad features and enormous noses, but their fortunes—estimated at hundreds of millions—made them attractive in the eyes of certain women.)

In *Stagestruck* (Harcourt, Brace and World, 1964) Maurice Zolotow relates incidents which took place at rehearsals for *Electra* in the **Greek Theatre** at Berkeley. Miss Anglin had cast Lunt to play the spirit of decadent Greece in a prologue to this play. At a dress rehearsal she protested that the actor looked far too innocent, too "normal" and not depraved enough. Lunt then pro‑ceeded to gild his hair and nipples, paint his fingernails and toenails red, and to drape vineleaves in his hair. He corraled two young male members of the company and painted them up likewise. He made his entrance at the next rehearsal as if drunk, embracing two Greek boys.

Rather daring stuff for 1915.

"I'm sure we shall all be arrested," said Miss Anglin, laughing. "But we will do it—though it is a bit more *fin de siècle* than I had in mind, Alfred."

At this point in his career, ugly or not, Alfred Lunt was appar‑ently irresistible to older actresses. Margaret Anglin passed him on to Laura Hope Crews, who hired him to play with her in a vaude‑ville sketch. Laura Hope Crews in turn bequeathed him to Lily Langtry, then fat and sixty-three but with a face that was still beauti‑ful. Langtry was a terrible actress, but when she needed money she played a season on the stage or in vaudeville. Lunt was her leading man in a sketch which opened at the **Orpheum Theatre** in San Francisco on September 7, 1916. (He was required, incidentally, to be a lover as well as leading man to all of these older ladies.) It was difficult enough to fake his passion while making love to Langtry, but Alfred was also expected to dance with her for hours before they—uh, performed the act, so to speak. Alfred did his best, but playing four shows a day was much less exhausting than satisfying Miss Langtry—who could have danced all night and, apparently, often did.

Alfred Lunt and Lynn Fontanne, as an acting team, played San Francisco on many occasions, notably in *The Taming of the Shrew* in 1939 and *The Great Sebastians* in the middle 50s. Alfred

22

once complained that the newer avant-garde playwrights, such as Beckett and Albee, never offered the Lunts their scripts. "They think the only plays we're interested in are light comedies, trifles by Noel Coward or Terence Rattigan." But actually the Lunts performed many works which were classics (Chekhov's *The Seagull*), experi - mental (O'Neill's *Strange Interlude*) or heavy drama (Maxwell An - derson's *Elizabeth the Queen*). Their very last performance was in Dürrenmatt's *The Visit*, a play and playwright which they in - troduced to American audiences and which must have given them great satisfaction as their farewell contribution to the theatre. *The Visit* was at the **Geary Theatre** with the Lunts in 1960.

During the 20s, 30s and 40s, as before, the great actors of the stage were encouraged to tour, not only to get additional mileage out of the vehicles in which they starred in New York but to build their reputations on a national level and to enlarge their fan followings. The theory was that if Mr. and Mrs. John Smith saw the Lunts in Kansas City and liked them then it was probable that the Smith family would buy tickets to whatever play the Lunts were doing on Broadway when they visited New York. There were some stars, too, the Lunts among them, who considered it a moral responsibility to go on tour, to help keep the theatre alive when talking pictures be - came popular, when playhouses were closed or being converted to film palaces, and when legitimate dramas on the stage were growing fewer.

As the days of the actor-managers bagan to fade, as the movies wooed many of Broadway's leading men and ladies to Hollywood, it was left to the likes of Ethel Barrymore, Katharine Cornell, Helen Hayes and a few others to carry the banner of live theatre and to take to the road, most often after they had completed successful runs with their plays in New York. Barrymore was in San Francisco with *Whiteoaks* and *The Corn Is Green* , both in the late 30s, and Helen Hayes was here in *Victoria Regina* and *Harriet* during the same period.

Katharine Cornell appeared in San Francisco in 1934, playing *Romeo and Juliet, Candida*, and *The Barretts of Wimpole Street* in repertory. In Oakland her company did all three plays in two days (two evening shows and a matinee) in an auditorium which was separated from a basketball court only by a thin partition. The ref - eree's whistle, says Tad Mosell in *Leading Lady* (Atlantic-Little, Brown, 1978) punctuated Mercutio's death and also the balcony scene. Cornell played Shaw's *St. Joan* and Behrman's *No Time for Comedy* in San Francisco, and she opened one play here, *Rose Burke*, which was not well received and which she decided not to take to New York but which was notable for introducing Jean-Pierre Aumont to American audiences. Cornell was appearing at the **Curran Theatre** in Shaw's *The Doctor's Dilemma* when Pearl Harbor was bombed in December, 1941 and, trouper that she was, she walked all the way down the hill from the **Fairmont** in a complete blackout on December 8 to play for her fans who had purchased tickets to the performance.

It was once said that Helen Hayes played queens as if they were women, while Katharine Cornell played women as if they were queens. There was often much controversy over which of these two women was First Lady of the American Stage. The only time the New York critics ever voted on this matter, Ethel Barry - more came out the winner. Howard Barnes, however, split his vote three ways: Barrymore for voice, Hayes for technique, Cornell for personality.

Tallulah Bankhead brought *The Little Foxes* on a tour which included San Francisco in its itinerary after the play's Broadway engagement, in 1939. Tallulah also appeared locally in a couple of her less distinguished efforts, *Dear Charles* and *Midgie Purvis*, as well as her long-running *Private Lives* which caused Noel Coward to say with a sigh, after he had caught a performance, "Well, it's not the same play Gertie (Lawrence) and I did in 1930, but it's making more money than it ever did, so I shouldn't complain."

Shirley Booth was in San Francisco with *Come Back, Little Sheba* and *The Desk Set*, both in the 50s. The inimitable Ruth Gordon played Thornton Wilder's *The Matchmaker* at the **Geary**, also in the 50s, several years before Broadway producer David Merrick turned that play into the renowned musical *Hello, Dolly!* Film stars Ginger Rogers and Miriam Hopkins, both of whom started their careers in the theatre, went back to the stage, respectively, in *The Pink Jungle* (a pre-Broadway tryout which never made it to New York) and Thomas Wolfe's *Look Homeward, Angel* (on tour after the Broadway run) which featured also in the cast a young actor named Keir Dullea who, only a few years before, had been a student at **San Francisco State** and whose role as the astronaut in the film *2001* was still ahead of him. Both of these productions were at the **Alcazar**, where Bette Davis also appeared with her (then) husband Gary Merrill in *The World of Carl Sandburg* in 1960. The lovely Vivien Leigh also made one of her rare San Francisco appearances in *Duel of Angels* at the **Alcazar** in 1960. Julie Harris, whom some believed would take over the throne of First Lady of the American Theatre, was in San Francisco a few times, the last many years ago in a weak **Theatre Guild** offering *The Warm Peninsula.*

Few of the great stage stars have brought their New York hits to San Francisco during the last two decades, and the reason for that is simple. There are few great stage stars left anymore and few who continue to appear in Broadway shows. Barrymore and Cornell are dead, Helen Hayes does movies and television films but has retired from the theatre, Noel Coward was here in the late 50s in *Present Laughter* and *Nude with Violin* but he's dead now, too; Alfred Lunt died a few years ago and so did Lynn Fontanne. The new breed of actor who scores a hit on Broadway may be willing to go on the road for a season or two (as Philip Anglim did in *The Elephant Man*) but can scarcely be considered a big star after one major success and usually opts to go immediately to Hollywood or into television where the money is, and then says good-bye to the theatre forever. A few exceptions, such as Al Pacino and Richard Dreyfuss, return to New York occasionally between films but they play only a few weeks in some off-Broadway house and seldom go on the road with their shows. While it's true that Burt Lancaster and Kirk Douglas were on the stage briefly before they went into films, they did not gain stardom on the stage. They are movie actors and their appearance at the **Marines Memorial Theatre** in San Fran - cisco a few years ago in *The Boys in Autumn* was a once-in-a- career event, a pre-Broadway tryout, and not part of a tour planned for its own sake. Hume Cronyn and Jessica Tandy were here with Anne Baxter in a bill of Noel Coward one-acts, but the Cronyns—fine actors though they are—have never enjoyed tremen - dous popular acclaim and have never had the fan following that, say, the Lunts or Katharine Cornell had in their heydays.

Those two big stars of the musical theatre, Ethel Merman and Mary Martin, both appeared in San Francisco many times—Merman in *Gypsy* in 1960, and Martin most notably in *South Pacific* and *Annie Get Your Gun* for the **Civic Light Opera** in the mid-50s. But Merman is dead and Martin semi-retired now. Carol Channing carries on. A native of San Francisco (she was a student at **Lowell**

High School) Channing brings a show to her old home town occasionally. She was here a few years ago with a pre-Broadway tour of *Lorelei*, a sort of sequel to her first big hit, *Gentlemen Prefer Blondes*. Channing and Martin teamed up in early 1986 to do a non-musical play called *Legends*.

Among the dramatic actresses, there are only two of the theatre's grandest dames still in there pitching and still willing to hit the road like the old-time troupers which they are. They nearly always include San Francisco in their itineraries.

Katharine Hepburn, who was a Broadway leading lady before she became a film star, has regularly returned to the theatre and, schooled in the old traditions, has considered the road a part of her job. She was in San Francisco as Rosalind in *As You Like It* in the early 50s, and she appeared here most recently in *A Matter of Gravity* and *West Side Waltz*. A star of the first magnitude (she was referred to by some of her *Waltz* company as "a national monu - ment") Hepburn is a great favorite and well-loved by audiences in the Bay area, where she always packs the house no matter how slight and inconsequential the play in which she is appearing.

Eva Le Gallienne is another great lady of the American stage, admired and respected by theatre people who appreciate the way she struggled over forty years to establish repertory in this country, and without the foundation grants which many regional theatres receive today. Le Gallienne has often appeared in San Francisco, with her Ibsen repertoire in 1939 (when audiences saw her famed modern dress version of *Hedda Gabler*) and her **National Repertory Theatre** in the mid-60s, which was the very last touring rep com - pany with major actors (Signe Hasso, Leora Dana, Sylvia Sidney, etc.) to perform in this city. Le Gallienne was here again in *The Royal Family* in 1977. The **Bay Area Theatre Critics Circle** gave her a special award at its annual ceremony in March, 1978.

Fritz Leiber was one of the last actor-managers of the old tradi - tion to play San Francisco in Shakespearean repertory. He was here in 1934—and the end of an era was marked when John Carradine appeared in *Hamlet*, *Othello* and *The Merchant of Venice* at the **Geary Theatre** in the autumn of 1943.

Carradine was a tall, thin, sonorous-voiced actor who had first attracted attention as something of an eccentric as he strolled Hollywood Boulevard in the early 1930s, dressed in a flowing cape and carrying a walking stick, reciting Shakespeare for anyone who would listen. Eventually, he won a small role in Cecil B. De Mille's *Sign of the Cross* and his career as a character actor in films was launched. (His sons David, Keith and Robert today frequently play romantic roles, but their father was always typed as a heavy in the movies and never played romantic leads.) Sometime during this period Carradine became a drinking buddy of John Barrymore, who was his idol and whom he often tried to emulate. By 1943 he had appeared in several outstanding films (among them *Stagecoach* and *The Grapes of Wrath*), his long-term contract with **Twentieth-Century Fox** was ended, and the actor decided to fulfill a dream of heading his own Shakespearean repertory company. He had saved his money, or enough of it, to finance this company and he was able to purchase the Robert Edmond Jones set which had been used in Barrymore's 1922 *Hamlet* production and which was up for sale after the Great Profile died. Carradine planned to use the Jones design as a unit set for his own productions of *Hamlet*, *Othello* and *The Merchant of Venice*.

I was engaged as a member of the Carradine company. Twenty-three at this time, I already had been working in the theatre and radio for six years. I had also just been discharged from the army and had scored a certain success in a play I had done at the **Geller Workshop**, the former **Max Reinhardt Studio** in Hol - lywood. On top of that, I had just been married to Maria Seiber, daughter of German film director Rudolph Seiber and his wife Marlene Dietrich. I was open to good job offers.

A friend told me that Carradine was casting for his company at the famed **Pasadena Playhouse**. I hurried over to Pasadena and read a few lines for Carradine, who complimented me and said that most of the major roles in his company, unfortunately, were already cast. There were only small parts open in *Hamlet* and *Othello*, but if I were willing to play them (on the chance that I might later step into the parts of Laertes and Cassio) he could offer me the role of Lorenzo, the romantic juvenile who elopes with Shylock's daughter Jessica in *The Merchant of Venice*. I was happy to accept this offer. The company, Carradine informed me, would play a few break-in performances in Pasadena and then move directly north to San Fran - cisco, where a two week stand at the **Geary Theatre** would mark the beginning of an extended tour. It was an exciting prospect. All of my early training had prepared me to play roles in the great classics (and I already had a few under my belt, as a matter of fact)

27

and I was delighted to have the opportunity to perform in the kind of theatre I loved.

Two or three days later an item appeared in Louella Parsons' column in the Los Angeles *Examiner* : "John Carradine didn't have any idea who Dean Goodman was when the young actor came to read for Carradine's Shakespearean company. 'All I knew,' says John, 'was that he could read Shakespeare and he had terrific legs for wearing tights.' "

Memories of the Carradine engagement in San Francisco, more than forty years ago, are still very clear to me. We opened the plays as planned, in Pasadena. ("*I* am playing Lorenzo beautifully to - night, my love!" said Maria in a note she sent to me backstage, letting me know that she was with me in spirit on the first night of *The Merchant of Venice*.) We came by train to Oakland, as everyone did in those days, and we crossed the Bay by ferry. It was an early October evening when we arrived; the air was crisp and cool and the city's skyline (without today's highrises) was a vivid and impres - sive sight. Here I was, fulfilling every actor's dream, opening in the glamorous city of San Francisco in a bona fide Shakespearean reper - tory company with a famous star! It was thrilling.

Carradine was in his element, too, as star of his own company. He played the old-time Shakespearean actor-manager role to the hilt, wearing his cape and hat and carrying his stick on the streets of every city we played throughout the tour, sometimes creating embarrassing scenes in restaurants ("Am I supposed to eat this—or did I?") all of it in emulation of his idol John Barrymore, and as if he were that actor's reincarnation. He reveled in the attention he was getting when he created a public scene or when an item about his eccentric behavior appeared in one of the newspapers. He loved to repeat Barrymore's famous line, when asked if he thought Hamlet were having an affair with Ophelia: "In my companies, gentlemen, she always did!" (And, in fact, Carradine *was* having an affair with Sonia Sorel, our company leading lady, and later married her.) I must say, though, that Carradine was always very kind to me and we worked together several times again in later years.

San Francisco received the Carradine company generously, and I had favorable reviews from the critics for my Lorenzo. We did good business at the **Geary**. I stayed at the **Somerton Hotel**, I re - member, just across the street from the theatre, and days were spent with other company members doing the things all first-time visitors to the city do—riding the cable cars, having lunch at Fisherman's Wharf, exploring Chinatown—and then rushing to the theatre for the evening's performance. Someday, I vowed, I would come back to this fabulous city to live and work. (It was a dozen years before I did, however.)

Carradine alternated with an actor named Alfred Allegro in the roles of Othello and Iago. He was much better in the latter role than as the Moor since, operating on the theory that the Moors were very cultured people, he played Othello in a very restrained dignified fashion. This doesn't work in a play which is about dark, passionate jealousy and must rise to great heights of emotion. Carradine's Hamlet had good moments—his "O, what a rogue and peasant slave am I!" soliloquy was particularly effective as he built it to a shat-tering climax—but it was as Shylock that the actor excelled. He made the old Jew both pitiable and sympathetic. It was my privilege to direct John in another production of *The Merchant of Venice*, over twenty years later, at Palo Alto's **Commedia Theatre** in 1965, and the old rascal (a chaser of his leading ladies to the end!) was as cunning as ever in the part.

Like many actors, however, Carradine was not a good busi-nessman, and his Shakespearean repertory company, started with such high hopes in 1943, played a few months on the road and then returned to Los Angeles for an engagement at the **Biltmore Theatre** while he tried to seek more financing and better bookings for the project. He was not successful and the company closed. Now almost eighty years old, Carradine still works as an actor (and has played Scrooge in *A Christmas Carol* in the Bay area) but I'm sure his fondest memory is of that autumn in 1943 when he played Hamlet, Othello and Shylock in San Francisco, Portland, Seattle and other major cities in Robert Edmond Jones's set for Barrymore's 1922 *Hamlet* on Broadway.

The seeds of San Francisco theatre as we now know it were probably planted with the **Federal Theatre Project**, devised and encouraged by Franklin Delano Roosevelt as part of his **National Recovery Act** during the 30s. The advent of sound to motion pictures, plus the impoverishment of the depression, had devastated the Bay area stage. Some local actors and technicians, lucky people that they were, were able to make a living through aid of the **Fed-**

eral Theatre. Touring shows still played the **Geary** and the **Alcazar**, and the **Civic Light Opera** was founded in 1935. Henry Duffy, whose stock company presented a new show every week, struggled through the 30s, until he finally departed for Los Angeles to open a school for aspiring actors.

A charming report from Jerald Elwood, now living in Carmel, reveals much about the climate of theatre in San Francisco during the perilous 30s. Elwood was co-director of the **Wayfarers Civic Repertory Theatre** founded by Jack Thomas in 1931.

"In 1931," says Elwood, "there was very little theatre in San Francisco. Occasional road shows came for a few weeks, Reginald Travers did something in the **Fairmont Hotel** now and then, and Ronald Telfer did a few productions at the **Western Women's Club** (now called the **Marines Memorial**) but that was it. The **Wayfarers** came into being out of frustration. Frustration of young people, from twenty to thirty years of age, who loved the theatre but had no theatre in which to pursue their love.

"An old loft was found at 74 Commercial Street, a half block from the Ferry building and the Embarcadero. It was all very primi - tive in the beginning. Our equipment was limited because our money was limited. Remember, the great Depression was on!

"The **Wayfarers** got no financial aid from any source. None of us got paid. We existed from the sale, advance sale mainly, of tickets to our subscribers. The fifty-cents-per-ticket sale was realistic in the 30s, because one could pay the same price to sit in the gallery downtown at one of the big theatres and see the Lunts or Katharine Cornell when they came to town!"

Elwood believes that the **Wayfarers** kept the theatre alive in San Francisco during the 1930s, because the company never stopped producing. The group never did a modern play; it couldn't afford to pay authors' royalties. Works of Shakespeare, Molière, Ibsen, Rostand, Gorki, Ben Jonson, Oscar Wilde, and the like were presented on weekends for four- or five-week runs. Eventually, in 1936, in a new home at 1749 Clay Street, the **Wayfarers** got into true repertory, performing plays in rotation Wednesday through Sat - urday for several weeks.

"Our concept of theatre," Elwood concludes, "was that there should be, in addition to a good production, an aura of mystery both behind and in front of the curtain. This we worked hard to achieve. We had candles on the walls of the auditorium and candle girls in

30

evening gowns to snuff them out when the gong sounded and the auditorium lights started slowly to dim, all accompanied by beautiful overture music. Our success finally was recognized nationally with pictures and articles in *Theatre Arts* and *Stage Magazine*, both of New York City. Our success, too, had been recognized by local drama critics such as George Warren, the dean of drama critics in San Francisco, John Hobart, Katherine Hill and Paul Speegle, all of the San Francisco *Chronicle*. Although other local papers covered us from time to time, it was the *Chronicle* that covered every produc - tion we did over a ten year period. The **Wayfarers** owed a great deal to the *Chronicle*, not only for its coverage including publicity but for the encouragement that came through in the critics' reviews. I have often thought that if it hadn't been for the *Chronicle*, we might not have had the success that we eventually enjoyed."

The **Wayfarers** closed up shop in 1941 with the coming of World War II and never reorganized. Other groups, however, began to form on the San Francisco scene after VJ Day.

One of these companies was the **San Francisco Municipal Theatre**, founded in 1946, which presented full seasons of plays at the **Marina Junior High School**, Chestnut and Fillmore Streets, for the next five years. A cursory glance at a program for *Strange Bedfellows*, a 1949 production, reveals the names of several theatre artists still active on the local scene, for example, one R. Martin Culp, better known to modern television viewers as Robert Culp. Leon Forbes, director of *Strange Bedfellows*, was later to direct and act for the **Actor's Workshop** and to serve as Artistic Director for another company, the **Interplayers**. Now semi-retired, Forbes currently plays character roles in many productions in the Los Gatos-Palo Alto area.

The **Interplayers**, also founded in 1946, began, as stated in a company biography prepared in 1953, with "four people, a small room and a play." The four people were Kermit Sheets, Martin Ponch, Joyce Lancaster and her husband Adrian Wilson. These four spent some six months working, rehearsing, and saving money to finance that play, "and the box-office receipts paid for the next play, thus enabling the group to begin its career without going into the red."

Lancaster, who played many leading roles with the **Inter - players**, also subsequently played a long run in Harold Pinter's *The Birthday Party* for the **Actor's Workshop**. She recalls the

31

early struggles of the former group. "There were no grants in those days, no special funding. We were entirely dependent upon box-office receipts for our subsistence. I think perhaps that made a great deal of difference in the dedication and devotion which we gave to our theatre. My experience in working with both professional and non-professional companies has led me to believe that people will do a great deal more for love than they will for money." It is her opin -ion that one of the problems with the local theatre scene today is that actors and other theatre artists are forced to turn into fundraisers. "Most theatre workers just aren't suited for this," she concludes.

The **Interplayers**, having no playhouse of their own, moved about considerably during the early years, performing at **Friends' Center**, the **Marines Memorial**, the **Palace of the Legion of Honor**, **Mills College**, a warehouse near Fisherman's Wharf (closed by the Fire Department after three performances), the **San Francisco Museum of Art**, then finally settled for a time in what the 1953 biography called "unique quarters in the old Verdier mansion" on Vallejo Street at Taylor. Shortly after, however, the company found more desirable headquarters at the **Bella Union Theatre** on Kearny Street (now a house screening Chinese films) and ultimately moved to a new home in a remodeled warehouse near **Rolf's Restaurant** on Beach Street, where it continued pro -ductions until the mid-1960s. The premises is now an art gallery.

In the 50s Loren Gage took over management of the **Inter -players** and was chief stage director of the company until his death in 1959, at which time Leon Forbes became the company's Artistic Director. Forbes enjoyed particular success with his versions of *The Matchmaker* and *Mrs. Warren's Profession*. He says, however, that his production of Arthur Miller's *A Memory of Two Mon -days* stands out in his mind. Brooks Atkinson, drama critic for the *New York Times*, saw the show on a trip to San Francisco and gave it a favorable review.

Among Gage's successes were Shaw's *St. Joan* and a produc -tion of *The Madwoman of Chaillot*, first performed at the Verdier mansion in 1953 and then later at the **Bella Union**. Joyce Lancas -ter played the role made famous on Broadway by Martita Hunt.

Lancaster's husband Adrian Wilson designed most of the pro -grams for the **Interplayers'** productions. Consummate works of art, they were eventually published in book form. The book is now out of print, a collector's item you can buy for $1,000 if you are

32

lucky enough to find a copy. Some of the original programs are on view in the San Francisco History room at the public library.

My own production of *Hamlet*, which I directed and for which the **Interplayers** gave me star billing, played for five weeks to sold-out houses in the spring of 1957. Gage and Lancaster played Polonius and Gertrude in this production. Martin Ponch and George Hitchcock, two other prominent **Interplayers** actors, were featured as the Ghost and Claudius, respectively. Alumni of the **Inter-players** who have recently been active in San Francisco and Bay area theatre include Kenna Hunt, who scored a great personal suc-cess in *The Couch* at the **Magic Theatre** in 1985, and William Wilson who has been seen in many **Lamplighter** productions.

A split occurred within the **Interplayers** in 1952. A segment of the company kept the name (those who went to the Verdier mansion) and a second segment formed a new company under the leadership of Kermit Sheets. This company was first called the **Playhouse Repertory Company** but came in time to be called simply the **Playhouse**. Sheets's followers remained in the plant at Beach and Hyde Streets, across from the **Buena Vista Restau-rant**, where a bar and restaurant operate today. The company, ac-cording to Sheets, "continued to present plays of substance in annual seasons of six main productions and occasional special events."

That playwrights such as Shaw, Ibsen, Chekhov, Giraudoux, Camus, Anouilh, Pirandello, Dürrenmatt, Garcia Lorca and Wede-kind often had their works produced at the **Playhouse** indicates the company's predilection for European theatre.

A production of *The Bald Soprano* introduced Ionesco and the Theatre of the Absurd to San Francisco. This was in 1956. Ameri-can theatre was represented by works of Mark Twain, Lynn Riggs, Lillian Hellman and Edward Albee, as well as by new scripts from San Francisco poets Madeline Gleason, James Broughton and Helen Adam, whose ballad opera *San Francisco's Burning*, with music by Warner Jepson, had one of the longest runs in **Playhouse** history.

Several alumni from Jasper Deeter's **Hedgerow Theatre** in Pennsylvania had a strong influence on the **Playhouse**, according to Sheets, in terms of plays chosen for production and standards of acting, directing, and production. Among those were Jane Steckle, one of the company's leading actresses, and Sydney Walker, until recently an active and much respected performer with the **American**

33

Conservatory Theatre. Other directors who helped form the **Playhouse** identity were Curtiss Cowan and Norma Miller.

"By 1970," says Sheets, "all of these company members had left the **Playhouse** to work elsewhere. That year the owner of the building decided to tear it down. A few more productions by younger members were produced under the **Playhouse** name around the city, but the company never survived the moves."

On Washington Street near Polk, in a space which is now a church, was a school called **Theatre Arts Colony**, which had operated for several years under the management of Arthur Gleditch. The producing team of Les Abbot and Les Abrams took over this comfortable and well-designed little theatre, with a seating capacity of about 200, in the mid-1950s and presented a series of com - mercially viable and yet dramatically effective Broadway hits such as *Dark of the Moon, Picnic, The Man with the Golden Arm, Tea and Sympathy* and various others. Will Marchetti, a fine actor still seen in many productions around the Bay area, was the young leading man of the Abbot-Abrams company. Later, these same producers leased the old **Encore Theatre** at 430 Mason Street, now the home of the **One Act Theatre Company**, where they presented several other shows, including André Gide's *The Immoralist*, starring Mar - chetti and Jocelyn Brando.

The **Theatre Arts Colony** building was subsequently taken over by the **Contemporary Dancers**, an experimental and highly controversial dance group which performed only sporadically and which, during the seasons of 1958-'60, sub-leased the space to the **Great Plays Company**, of which I was the Artistic Director and producer. Over a period of three years the **Great Plays Company** presented thirteen shows, ranging in variety from Strindberg's *The Father* to Herman Wouk's *The Caine Mutiny Court Martial* to the first local production of Jean Genet's *The Maids*, and to such musicals as *Good News* and *One Touch of Venus*. The company also enjoyed a great success with the first San Francisco production of Rattigan's *Separate Tables*. Dianne Feinstein, performing under her maiden name of Dianne Goldman, made her only known local appearance as a stage actress playing Hilda Wangel opposite my Solness in Ibsen's *The Master Builder*. Feinstein is today, of course, better known as the mayor of San Francisco. Joel Fabiani, recently seen as Joan Collins' great friend King Gaylen on tele -

vision's *Dynasty*, made his first stage appearance here in the **Great Plays Company** production of *Career*.

Highly stylized productions with exceptionally beautiful cos - tumes were the forte and claim to fame of the **Company of the Golden Hind** which, under the leadership of Rachmel ben Avram, flourished in Berkeley during the late 1950s. Ben Avram subse - quently moved his company to the **Little Fox Theatre** in San Francisco's North Beach area where, departing from his Berkeley policy of presenting more classical works of playwrights such as Molière and Wilde, he offered productions of the popular musicals *The Boy Friend* , *Oh, Captain!* and *House of Flowers*. Ben Avram still lives and works in San Francisco but has not been active in the theatre for some time.

Probably the best known and most successful producer of musicals on the local scene, at least on a modest economical basis, was a woman named Irma Kay who, for several seasons, managed the **Opera Ring** on South Van Ness Avenue. Kay presented such diverse shows as *Guys and Dolls* and *Once upon a Mattress*, among a score of others. Her featured performers included Diane Berman and Harry Grilley, who until recently operated and per - formed at the **Sea Witch**, a bistro in Ghirardelli Square. Although the **Opera Ring** made its reputation with musicals, there were oc - casional dramatic shows presented in its theatre-in-the-round space. The first San Francisco production of John Osborne's *Look Back in Anger*, for example, was staged at this location. Manager Irma Kay closed her theatre in the 60s and moved to Marin County where at last report she was operating as a theatrical agent.

A partnership composed of Keith Rockwell, John Guttierez and Arthur Meyer leased space on Broadway which had been an after-hours coffee house, redecorated it, turned it into a 399 seat theatre called the **On Broadway**, and produced shows of their own there for several years. (Rockwell and Meyer had previously been producers of a successful long-run production of *The Fantasticks* in Ghirardelli Square.) Then, for a time, the theatre was leased to inde - pendent producers. Many long-run **Equity** shows played in this theatre, everything from *Norman, Is That You?* to the comedy-drama *The Trial of James McNeill Whistler* to musicals such as *All Night Strut* and the 1980-'81 hit *Stompin' at the Savoy*. The **On Broadway** is now a rock and roll disco.

35

Rockwell also bought fixtures from the elegant Fox movie theatre on Market Street (where the **Fox Plaza** now stands) when it was torn down in the early 60s, and used them to create the **Little Fox,** a theatre on Pacific Street. For the next fifteen years a wide variety of productions played in this house, most notably *One Flew Over the Cuckoo's Nest,* which ran for five years. In the middle 70s Francis Ford Coppola bought the premises and announced plans for his own repertory company. These plans never materialized and no other productions have been booked into the **Little Fox** for some time now.

Randolph Hale operated the **Alcazar** on O'Farrell Street during the 1950s, frequently booking in touring shows but also presenting long runs of his own, many of which featured his wife Marjorie Lord, who gained greater fame as Danny Thomas's wife in a television series called *Make Room for Daddy.* The beautiful **Alcazar,** thought by many to be the most attractive playhouse in the city, was torn down in 1963 to make room for a parking lot. A new **Alcazar** was opened by Keith Rockwell, Roger Williams and a group of partners at 650 Geary Street in the early 70s. The lobby of this theatre displayed posters of many of the productions which played the older **Alcazar** during its heyday. The new **Alcazar** housed more than its share of failures, but Dick Shawn's *The Second Greatest Entertainer in the World,* the **Eureka Theatre**'s *Cloud Nine,* and a two-man show called *Greater Tuna* were notable hits at this location. The theatre is now dark, undergoing renovation.

Both the **Lamplighters** and the **San Francisco Mime Troupe** had their beginnings in the 1950s. The former produces mainly Gilbert and Sullivan operettas in a permanent theatre; the latter does its plays in parks and auditoriums throughout the city and goes on extended tours. Since both of these companies are still in existence, they will be discussed in a later chapter.

In the field of modern drama, it was the **Actor's Workshop** which made the greatest impression on San Francisco audiences and, for a period of almost fifteen years, dominated the serious theatre scene on the local level. Starting in a small studio on Elgin Street in 1951, this company was founded and managed by Jules Irving and Herbert Blau, a pair of idealistic young professors at **San Francisco State University**. In any hindsight analysis of this partnership, most people who knew them will concede that Blau was the intellect of the two, the iconoclast whose influence and choice of plays were daring enough to bring the **Workshop** to national attention, but it was Irving whose warmth and personal charm held the company together on a day-to-day basis. If Blau was the brains, Irving was the heart of the San Francisco **Actor's Workshop**.

"I was in a position to help Jules in quite a few ways when he was getting started," recalls Leon Forbes. "Aside from loving the guy, I felt he had great potential for the theatre. I was able to play a few parts for the **Workshop** and directed one of their hits, *The Country Wife*, as a studio production at the **Bella Union Theatre**."

The **Workshop** went through three or four seasons at Elgin Street, struggling to survive all of the problems which confront any young theatre company, often playing to small audiences and not being taken too seriously by press and public. Gradually, however, with the aid of their wives, Priscilla Pointer and Beatrice Manley, Irving and Blau began to attract better actors and production standards improved. In the fall of 1955 the company moved into the **Marines Memorial Theatre** with the rather safe (for them) production of Wilde's *The Importance of Being Earnest*, after a smash hit with Arthur Miller's *The Crucible* at Elgin Street finally convinced local audiences that this was a group with real profes - sional standards.

It was not all smooth sailing, however, even after that. The company was highly controversial and always in trouble financially. Though the **Workshop** can take credit for introducing the plays of Harold Pinter, Samuel Beckett and Edward Albee to San Francisco audiences (*The Birthday Party* and a double bill of *Krapp's Last Tape* and *The Zoo Story* each ran for a solid year at the **Encore**, which the company took over for its more experimental productions) the general theatregoing public often found Blau's choice of plays too esoteric and his productions too peculiarly staged for popular success. The **Workshop's** audience was a cult audience and con - sidered by many to be elitist. There can be no doubt, however, that the **Workshop** laid the ground for a new kind of theatre in San Francisco.

When in 1960 the **Workshop** received a grant from the **Ford Foundation**, it was one of the first in the country to receive such monies. A group of actors was signed to **Equity** contracts to form a resident company and other actors were jobbed in from play to play for special roles. From time to time, guest directors such as Alan Schneider and William Ball were imported to direct particular pro - ductions.

In 1965 Blau and Irving received an offer to manage **Lincoln Center** in New York. They accepted. There was much consterna - tion when it was announced that they would be leaving San Fran - cisco, not only amid the audience which they had developed and their board of directors who had supported them but among many of their actors who felt that the two men were, in a sense, betraying a trust and a dedication to the development of a truly fine theatre company in San Francisco. But perhaps Blau and Irving's "deser - tion" was inevitable. Even after fifteen years, the **Workshop** had not achieved the goals which the directors had set for it. They felt the public attitude toward the company was apathetic, and they were discouraged. "We had reached the point of diminishing returns," Irving said later, in explanation of the pair's departure, "in which we really couldn't take any step forward. It was beyond survival."

Blau and Irving took many of the company's leading actors with them to New York to work at **Lincoln Center**. Michael O'Sullivan and Edward Winter were among those who achieved success, not only at **Lincoln Center** but in other roles on Broad - way. Robert Symonds, a leading actor with the **Workshop** here, directed and acted at **Lincoln Center** and may now be seen occa - sionally on television and in films. (He played the judge in *Kramer vs. Kramer* and is the spokesman in the current Hallmark Cards commercials on television.) Blau discovered the **Lincoln Center** climate not to his liking and soon resigned to return to teaching. Irving remained in his post until 1973 and then went to Hollywood where he produced films for television until his death in 1979.

Other actors who were with the **Workshop** during its heyday and who may be seen in films or on television include Irving's ex-wife Priscilla Pointer (now married to Robert Symonds) who had a featured role on *Dallas* for a time and has appeared with her daugh - ter Amy Irving in two of the latter's films, Eugene Roche, Tom Rosqui, Robert Phalen and Erica Speyer. Elizabeth Huddle, for many years a leading actress with the **American Conservatory Theatre** in San Francisco and now Artistic Director of the **Intiman Theatre** in Seattle, Washington, played her first important roles with the **Workshop** and was with Irving and Blau for a season at **Lincoln Center**. Robert Haswell and his wife Shirley Jac Wagner also accompanied the two directors to New York; these performers have been seen most recently with the **Berkeley Repertory Theatre**. Joseph Miksak, Winifred Mann, Irving Israel and I are still other actors who played important roles with the **Workshop** and are still active on the San Francisco-Bay area theatre scene.

After Blau and Irving left, an attempt was made to keep the **Workshop** alive. John Hancock was the director brought here to help salvage the company and a man named Ken Kitch tried to help him. They lasted a season or so and then announced that they were leaving for Pittsburgh, where they had received a better offer. The **Workshop** finished a season at the **Marines Memorial**, then closed, and thus ended an era.

For a short while things looked very bleak indeed, both for theatre workers and theatregoers. The **Workshop** was gone and so were most of the smaller companies described earlier in this section.

However, as the sages have observed, when one door closes another usually opens. It may take a little time to be noticed, but the ending of one era signifies the beginning of another. Few people were aware of it in 1966, but San Francisco was on the brink of a brilliant theatrical renaissance, an era that may go down in history as the most productive and exciting period the city has ever known.

2

IN THE A.C.T.

In 1967, like a galaxy of stars exploding over the city and setting fire to the sky, came William Ball with his **American Conservatory Theatre**, first for a short season and then subse - quently to remain in San Francisco. Within a brief time, **A.C.T.** had won acclaim and recognition as one of the two or three top re - gional theatre companies in the United States. In the Bay area, no other permanently based theatre group has ever had the critical and popular success that **A.C.T.** has now enjoyed for twenty years.

In early 1986 William Ball announced his resignation as gen - eral director of **A.C.T.** Within a few days Edward Hastings was announced as Ball's replacement. There will be more about this turn of events in later chapters.

A.C.T. opened its first season in Pittsburgh with Ball's pro - duction of *Tartuffe* on July 15, 1965. After a series of short-term bookings, the company made its western debut at **Stanford Uni - versity** in July, 1966. This brought about an offer from the San Francisco **Chamber of Commerce** to become this city's resident theatre company. The first season, presenting sixteen productions in repertory at the **Geary** and **Marines Memorial** theatres, opened

40

on January 21, 1967 with *Tartuffe* and continued through June 18 of that year.

San Franciscans were dazzled by Ball's imaginative stagings, not only of Molière's *Tartuffe* but also of Edward Albee's *Tiny Alice* and Pirandello's *Six Characters in Search of an Author*. The ensemble playing of the company's actors was labelled brilliant.

Original plans were for the company to play an annual season in Chicago as well as San Francisco, but during the spring of 1967 the Chicago season became an increasingly uncertain prospect. Suf - ficient support was rallied to keep the company permanently in the Bay area, and San Francisco has remained the company's home since that time. Periodically, rumors circulate that Ball and his pres - tigious group might go on an extended tour or accept an offer to move to another city, but to date neither of these things has hap - pened.

"Little did we realize on the opening night of *Tartuffe* in January of 1967 that the closing night, a few months later, would cement a long-term love affair between a city and a theatre com - pany," wrote actor Ken Ruta in **A.C.T.**'s tenth anniversary book. "My six seasons were the happiest years of my life and the most fruitful of my career. The successes, basking in them, and the fail - ures, learning from them. My memories of these times are multi - tudinous, but some will stay with me forever."

A.C.T. has indeed supplied a home and a consequent sense of comparative stability to its actors, technicians and administrative personnel. While many of its most prominent directors, such as Ellis Rabb, Tom Moore and Nagle Jackson, have jobbed in for the occa - sional play and then left to direct elsewhere, and while such actors as Michael Learned, Marc Singer, Marsha Mason, David Dukes and Paul Shenar have gone on to work on Broadway, with different regional theatres and in films and television, still other directors (such as Allen Fletcher, Edward Hastings and Ball himself) and other actors (including Elizabeth Huddle, William Paterson, Raye Birk, Ray Reinhardt, Barbara Dirickson, Marrian Walters, Anne Lawder, Dakin Matthews and Sydney Walker) have chosen to remain with the company for extended periods of time. A few per - formers such as Ruth Kobart have left the company for other engagements and then returned to the fold. Peter Donat, as another example, has been able to appear in two or three plays with **A.C.T.** each season and yet accept film and television offers, concurrently

41

or in-between. Part of Ball's original philosophy in founding the company was that artists should be able to leave the nest and try their wings elsewhere, then be welcomed home again when they desire to return, as Joy Carlin has done.

An integral part of **A.C.T.** and Ball's concept of a conservatory theatre is the belief that it is the responsibility of the actor to pass on his general knowledge to younger members of the profession, to conserve in the literal meaning of the word, "to keep from being damaged, lost or wasted." In addition to training for company members, **A.C.T.** offers full-time instruction to carefully selected young people who come to San Francisco from many parts of the country for the company's two year Advanced Training program, taught by **A.C.T.**'s most prominent actors and directors.

The company has usually conducted an annual ten week Summer Training Congress, an evening extension class each spring, and a Young Conservatory with a general introduction to the world of theatre for children from nine through eighteen years of age. A bulletin detailing the professional training programs at **A.C.T.** may be obtained by writing to the Conservatory at 450 Geary Street, San Francisco, California 94102.

New plays have also been a part of the **A.C.T.** idea. Although a few new works have been presented at the **Geary** and the **Marines Memorial**, the need to fill large houses soon limited the company's ability or willingness to take chances. Some critics have taken Ball and the company to task for this. The impulse to work with new writers remains, however, and many new plays have been presented under the Plays-In-Progress program, instituted in 1972. Here writers have the opportunity to see their plays presented under ideal workshop conditions, with limited production budgets but directed and performed by leading members of the **A.C.T.** company. In response to those who still criticize the company for a "conservative" choice of plays and an unwillingness to take risks, it should be pointed out that the 1985-'86 season featured at least three productions which were either new, and therefore chancy, or non-commercial. Only *Opéra Comique* by Nagle Jackson was both a critical and popular success.

At the **Marines Memorial** on Sutter at Mason Street, **A.C.T.** has occasionally sponsored presentations of independent productions. In 1981 Sam Shepard's *True West* and the touring version of the Broadway success *Children of a Lesser God* were examples of such projects.

During the summers, **A.C.T.** has frequently taken shows to Hawaii and Alaska. Tours to Russia, Japan and China have also enhanced the company's international reputation and proved to be rewarding experiences for the actors, directors and technicians lucky enough to be included.

The goals that Ball established in 1965 are still the force behind **A.C.T.** today. The company draws its repertory from the classics of dramatic literature, outstanding works of modern theatre, and the latest and best from New York and London. For many years the plays were presented in the rotating style of continental repertory and audiences could choose, in any given week, to see on the **Geary** stage such diverse works as Chekhov's *The Three Sisters*, Stoppard's *Night and Day*, and Lillian Hellman's *Another Part of the Forest*. Economics have made it necessary, in recent seasons, to present the plays in individual runs rather than in rotation, but all plays are not only exquisitely acted but staged with the most brilliant settings and light designs to be seen anywhere in the country.

In 1974, with support from the **Ford Foundation, A.C.T.** was able to purchase the **Geary Theatre** through a lease arrange - ment and thereby be assured of its permanent home. The company has official non-profit corporate status and receives grants from a long list of foundations, as well as funds from private and organiza - tional donors. While the company plays to better than ninety percent capacity at the **Geary**, there is still a deficit each year due to the tremendous expense of maintaining such an ambitious program. Box-office receipts alone cannot satisfy the total financial need. The **California Association for A.C.T.** attempted for many years to cover the season's deficits and to guarantee the budget for the coming year.

The press was extremely supportive of the company during its first decade. Then, as a new breed of drama editors arrived on the San Francisco scene, reviewers and reporters grew more and more critical of **A.C.T.** and of Ball and his administrative policies. Some published reports, such as one which suggested a mishandling of funds, was proved unfounded and unfair when an audit of the com - pany's books showed all financial matters to be in order. A few major critics, guided by questionable motives, continued to belittle

A.C.T. at every opportunity and seemed, at times, to be conduct - ing a personal vendetta against William Ball himself.

Nevertheless, any honest study of the past will reveal that **A.C.T.** occupies a unique shrine in the history of San Francisco theatre. There has never been a fully professional theatre company which has enjoyed such local support, achieved the international recognition and acclaim, and has lasted as long in the Bay area as **A.C.T.** has done. Despite the problems it faces, and these are problems not unlike those which face any theatre company regard - less of size or status, there is every likelihood that **A.C.T.** will con - tinue its reign in San Francisco for a long time to come under the able guidance of its new general director Edward Hastings.

Jules Irving and Herbert Blau, co-directors of the Actor's Workshop.
(Photo: Edward Winter)

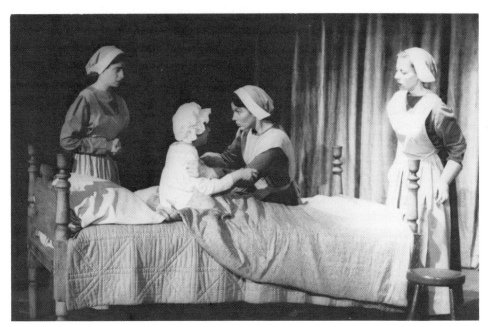

Scene from Actor's Workshop's *The Crucible*, 1955-'56 (above). Child is Karen Kondazian, with Priscilla Pointer on bed beside her.

Ensemble scene from Actor's Workshop's *The Crucible*, 1955-'56 (below), with Jules Irving as John Proctor standing second from left. (Photos: Pointer Collection)

Loren Gage (director) and Joyce Lancaster (leading lady) pause during a rehearsal for *The Madwoman of Chaillot*, an Interplayers production, 1954 (facing page). (Photo: Lancaster Collection)

Viveca Lindfors and Joseph Miksak were leading players in *Miss Julie*, an Actor's Workshop production, 1956-'57 season. (Photo: Miksak Collection)

Dianne Goldman (later Feinstein) was Hilda Wangel, and Dean Goodman was Solness in *The Master Builder*, a Great Plays Company production, 1959. (Photo: Goodman Collection)

TheAlchemist

Directed by Robert Loper

Lighting by	Sets by	Costumes by
James McMillan	Robert La Vigne	Roger le Cloutier

CAST OF CHARACTERS

Subtle	Michael O'Sullivan
Face	Robert Symonds
Dol Common	Peggy Doyle
Dapper	William Major
Drugger	Ray Fry
Sir Epicure Mammon	Dean Goodman
Surly	Albert Paulsen
Ananias	Dwight Frye
Tribulation Wholesome	Dion Chesse
Kastril	Joel Fabiani
Dame Pliant	Libby Glenn
Lovewit	Laurence Hugo
Neighbors	Joe Bellan, Pam Maudsley, Katharine Ross, David O'Neill, Morgan Upton, James Donohue
Officers	David O'Neill, James Dohohue
Parson	Joe Bellan

Program copy from the Actor's Workshop production of *The Alchemist*, 1960, lists names of artists who have had enduring careers.

Director Robert Loper is now active in Seattle theatre; lighting designer James McMillan is current manager of the Regency III movie house in San Francisco. Actors Michael O'Sullivan, Robert Symonds and Ray Fry accompanied Irving and Blau to Lincoln Center in New York; O'Sullivan returned here to work with A.C.T. and is now deceased, Symonds works in films and television, and Fry was last reported with the Actors' Theatre in Louisville. Dean Goodman is author of this book, Albert Paulsen has played villains in films and television, Dion Chesse appeared for a season with A.C.T. and was last seen in a play at the Magic, and Laurence Hugo has appeared in several plays off-Broadway and in television. Katharine Ross has most recently appeared on television's *The Colby's*, while Joel Fabiani (who was Ross's husband when they were with the Workshop) played Joan Collins' friend King Gaylen on *Dynasty*. Joe Bellan and Morgan Upton are still active in San Francisco theatre and have appeared in plays at the Magic, the Eureka and the One Act.

Pictured in the ruins of the razed Alcazar Theatre on O'Farrell Street in 1963 are several artists who participated in a May Festival at The Playhouse. Left to right: Pianist Thomas Hutchings, harpist Joel Andrews, poet James Broughton, actress Libby Glenn, technical designer Robert Wrobel, designer Eliza Pietsch, composer Warner Jepson, poet Helen Adam; director Kermit Sheets, designer Jo Landor, choreographer Anna Halprin and lighting designer Patrick Hickey. (Photo: Chester Kessler)

Winifred Mann and Tennessee Williams confer during rehearsal of *The Milk Train Doesn't Stop Here Anymore*, an Actor's Workshop production, 1966. (Photo: Baron Wolman)

3

MUSIC BY SUBSCRIPTION

For forty-five years the **San Francisco Civic Light Op-era**, first under the direction of Edwin Lester and then finally under the producing team of Feuer and Martin, provided theatregoers with a regular series of musicals at the **Curran** and **Orpheum** theatres. The biggest Broadway shows and the most luminous of inter-national stars were seen on these stages. Then, at the finish of the 1981 season, the producing directors announced that the company was storing its sets, packing away its costumes and props, and clos-ing its doors forever.

Why?

There appeared to be several reasons for the demise of the **CLO**. The last couple of subscription series weren't too well received. *Evita* was a smash hit, but half-hearted successes like *On the Twentieth Century* and *Umbrellas of Cherbourg*, and bombs like a revival of *Guys and Dolls* starring Milton Berle didn't bring customers rushing to the box-office. Not enough customers, anyway, to compensate for the last minute cancellation of 1981's supposed-to-be blockbuster *Gypsy* starring Debbie Reynolds. It was reported that guarantors weren't too happy, either, about being

45

called on to make up the company's deficits, something which hadn't happened too often in the past. The **CLO** shows played six weeks in Los Angeles as well as six weeks in San Francisco, but rising production costs reached the point where they didn't enable a musical to pay off its initial investment in such a limited playing time. There was talk that the **CLO** might add bookings in other cit - ies and develop a larger playing circuit. But this didn't happen. No further subscription series were announced, and the **CLO** did indeed close up shop.

Probably a strong reason, too, for the decline and disinte - gration of the **CLO** was the emergence of a dynamic and exceed - ingly shrewd new impresario on the San Francisco scene. Her name was Carole Shorenstein. Supported by family money, this young lady rocked the town back on its heels and made her detractors eat their words by bringing such top-flight musicals into local theatres that she has since practically eliminated all competition.

In 1986 Shorenstein is still a controversial figure in San Fran - cisco. Some of her critics point out that she doesn't do much for San Francisco artists. She doesn't produce new shows locally, using Bay area talent. She brings in package shows from out of town, usually with big-name stars, shows which are already proven suc - cesses. They say she's difficult to work for and very demanding of the employees in her San Francisco office. But whatever "they" say, there can be no doubt about it. Carole Shorenstein is the lady to reckon with on today's musical theatre scene in this part of the country.

Shorenstein went into partnership with James Nederlander in 1978 to begin a "Best of Broadway" series at the **Curran Theatre** in December of that year. In December, 1979, she opened the refur - bished **Golden Gate Theatre** which in the season of 1980-'81 housed the smash hit productions of *My Fair Lady* with Rex Har - rison and *Camelot* with Richard Burton. When the **CLO** gave up the **Orpheum**, Shorenstein took over the theatre, too. She installed a new sound system and and started booking attractions into this lo - cation at Eighth and Market Streets. *A Chorus Line*, the fourth time around, still packed them in at the **Golden Gate** in the late spring and early summer of 1981.

Asked which of her shows she considered the most successful, Shorenstein was hard put to give an answer. *La Cage aux folles* and *Forty-Second Street* have been recent box-office bonanzas.

46

"They've all been successful, really. Both artistically and finan -
cially."

Even *Sweeney Todd*?

"Yes, even *Sweeney Todd*. I loved that show. There have been
reports that the production lost money here and we had to close
early. That's not quite true. We did close earlier than we had origin -
ally planned, but it was because we saw that the box-office returns
were falling off and we wanted to close before we did lose money.
So you can't say that *Sweeney Todd* was a failure here. We closed
when we were still ahead."

(Sources close to the production assert that two unfavorable
reviews by Gerald Nachman in the San Francisco *Chronicle* hurt
the business for *Sweeney Todd* and resulted in the early closing.)

It is Shorenstein's opinion that most Broadway producers
don't understand the road. But they're beginning to learn. "They
used to think of San Francisco as a four to six week run for a show.
Now we play a show for nine or ten weeks. We've got the largest
subscription audience in the United States, and that means the larg -
est in the world. The Broadway producers are beginning to appreci -
ate that. Now they all want to book their shows into my theatres or
try out new productions here before they take them on to New
York."

Carole Shorenstein has proved that if the public is offered a
good product the people will buy it. Her record seems to substan -
tiate her philosophy. In recent seasons she has not limited herself to
musicals but has also brought in straight dramas such as *Glengarry
Glen Ross* and other plays which have found particular audiences in
San Francisco.

Will she invest in future Broadway productions?

"Yes, indeed."

No matter what her detractors say about her, probably as much
out of envy as anything else, this lady must be doing a few things
right. She appears to have found a formula which is working. No
independent producer based in San Francisco has ever been quite so
successful. With rare exceptions, Carole Shorenstein's three big the -
atres play to packed houses nightly, proof that audiences will still
support music-by-subscription in the 1980s as they did in the 1930s
when Edwin Lester started his **Civic Light Opera** series.

4

WAIVERS AND SMALL PROFESSIONAL THEATRES

Recognizing the need of professional actors to tone their muscles, remain in form and to practice their skills between paid engagements, and also recognizing the need for actors in certain areas to be seen by producers and directors in roles they might otherwise have little chance to play, a ninety-nine seat waiver plan was implemented in the Los Angeles and San Francisco regions in 1972. Created by the rank and file members of **Equity** and not as some have believed by the union's paid staff members, the 1972 rule states:

> Actors Equity will waive all Equity rules in theatres not capable of, or ever having had, seating facilities for more than ninety-nine people in the Los Angeles and San Francisco areas covered by the Hollywood/Bay Area Theatre contract. This waiver will not include any theatre operating as a Cafe, Dinner, or Children's Theatre. A Subsidiary Rights Agreement must be filed with the Equity office for all original plays.

What this rule meant, in effect, was that professional **Equity** actors could appear in small theatre productions without a union contract, with the knowledge that they did so at their own risk and that **Equity** could not protect them in conventional ways since union rules had been waived. It is important to note, however, that **Equity** did not relinquish jurisdiction over such theatres nor its right to decide which theatres qualified for the waiver and which did not, nor its right to place any management on probation or withdraw its waiver altogether if the basic ninety-nine seat rule was violated or if actors complained of mistreatment. Implicit in the agreement, also, was the understanding that since actors were performing without a standard contract they were free to leave a given production at any time, with or without notice. This policy was better understood in Los Angeles, where waiver theatres operated more as showcases and where actors might get a television or film assignment which required their immediate presence, but San Francisco actors were permitted to leave shows also for paying jobs (since the waiver houses seldom paid performers more than transportation expenses, if that) or for other personal reasons. Naturally, not all producers and directors were happy about this policy, but it was one of the risks they took if they chose to operate under the union waiver and use certain actors.

The ninety-nine seat limitation was admitted by **Equity** to be an arbitrary one, but the figure was adopted because the consensus of the membership was that no management with a theatre seating ninety-nine people or less would be likely to show much profit; the management therefore could not be guilty of exploiting professional actors for its own commercial gain.

The waiver plan became increasingly controversial, both among **Equity** actors and among the theatre managements, particu - larly in the San Francisco area. **Equity**'s paid staff members never favored the plan. They contended that they spent more time dealing with problems connected with the waiver theatres, which paid actors little or no money, than they did in settling disputes in contract pro - ductions from which actors earned a living wage.

A strong bone of contention and the cause of much heated con - troversy has always been the **Subsidiary Rights Agreement**. This clause in the waiver rule was instituted to protect **Equity** actors who contributed their time and talent, with little or no recompense, to the development of new scripts which are tried out in waiver houses. The union membership took the position that a professional actor who works without pay to develop a new script deserves to be paid for the work, in one way or another, if the play is picked up by a producer for a full professional production. The actor often makes a vital contribution to the development of a script, suggests changes, and enables the playwright to see the work come alive and find out which scenes need revision and which do not. The membership ruled that it is only fair, as recompense for this contribution, for the actor to have first refusal of his/her original role if the play goes to contract production.

If, for whatever reason, the actor decides not to accept the part in the contract production, then everybody is relieved of further responsibility, it was determined. But while the new management is not obligated to hire the actor in question, it is obligated to pay him or her four weeks' rehearsal salary at union scale if it does not. **Equity** stated repeatedly that this obligation rests with the producer of the professional production, and not the original waiver house producer. It was stressed that, no matter what happens, the professional producer has had an inexpensive tryout of the script in the waiver theatre and that the payoff to the original actor is small potatoes and only fair.

Over the years some waiver house managements had no problems dealing with the **SRA**; others objected strongly. Members of the **Dramatists' Guild** in New York filed suit against **Equity**, claiming that enforcement of the **SRA** was unfair labor practice and could perhaps prevent the sale of a new play for contract production since a producer might be unwilling to accept the lien. **Equity** claimed there was no record of any producer refusing a script in which he or she was interested because of the **SRA**.

Eventually in 1985 as part of negotiations for a new **LORT (League of Resident Theatres)** contract it was agreed that a special fund, to which all waiver and showcase theatres that produce original plays must contribute, would be established to pay off **Equity** actors who appeared in the tryouts and were not hired for the full professional productions.

For many years **Equity** had a paid representative in San Francisco who handled local union business mainly out of his home. In the middle 1960s, however, office space was rented by the union from a law firm at 100 Bush Street. In the middle 1970s there was talk of the **Equity Council** in New York closing the San Francisco office and dismissing Kathy Ewers, the law firm employee who handled **Equity** affairs. In protest against this threatened action, an ad hoc committee of **Equity** members was formed and this commit - tee did indeed convince Equity's **Western Advisory Board** and the **Council** in New York to maintain the office and to retain a paid staff member in San Francisco. Kathy Ewers eventually resigned and her post was taken by Jay Moran, a former **Equity** stage mana - ger. In 1986 Moran is still the **Equity** representative for this area. He works out of an office shared with the **Screen Actors' Guild**, also at 100 Bush Street.

The **Western Advisory Board** in Los Angeles and **Coun - cil** in New York saw the wisdom of establishing an advisory committee for **Equity** business in and around San Francisco. An election was held at a general membership meeting in March, 1977 and the first **Bay Area Advisory Committee** was formed. This committee was mandated to include ten principal actors and one chorus member. It was to hold an official meeting at least once a month with the local staff member and Edward Weston, Western Regional Director of **Equity**, in attendance. The committee's func - tion was, and remains to this day, solely advisory to staff and the **WAB** and **Council**.

At the meeting at the **St. Francis Hotel** in March, 1977, the following members were elected to serve on the first officially rec - ognized **Bay Area Advisory Committee** (although there had been another committee which operated briefly in the middle 1960s): Roberta Callahan, Ruth Kobart, Francine Forest, Dakin Matthews, Dean Goodman, Jay Leo Colt, Wayne Alexander, Adele Proom, Janice Garcia, and J. C. Forman. The seat designated for the chorus member was left unfilled, as it has remained in most subsequent elections.

BAAC was charged to elect its own officers, and those elected for the first year's term were: Dean Goodman, Chairperson; Fran - cine Forest, 1st Vice-Chairperson; Jay Leo Colt, 2nd Vice-Chair - person; and Adele Proom, Recording Secretary.

One of the sub-committees established by the newly elected Chairperson, was the Waiver House sub-committee, first headed by Adele Proom. In pairs and trios, **BAAC** members visited the several operating waiver houses to explain the rules to managements and also to encourage the more prominent companies to include salaries for actors in their annual budgets.

51

Although **Equity**'s paid staff never particularly liked the waiver plan, and although a few actors opposed it, every time the issue was put to a vote in San Francisco and Los Angeles the mem - bership elected to continue the waiver. Most actors have recognized the creative opportunities they receive in waiver houses, and they have also recognized the contribution that these theatres make by introducing new plays and playwrights and by producing works ne - glected in the commercial theatre.

But in the beginning, when the ninety-nine seat limitation was placed on seating capacity, nobody thought that the waiver theatres would have any source of revenue except box-office receipts, and these receipts (actors believed) wouldn't ordinarily be large enough to merit salaries for performers. Everybody believed the waiver theatres would remain, more or less, workshops or showcases for actors.

Then some of the waiver house managements secured non-profit corporate status, became eligible for foundation grants and began to operate on larger budgets. Some of these annual budgets reached sums of $300,000 to $400,000. Managers and publicity people were being paid a living wage, as were many technicians and directors, but actors still received little more than lunch money. Performers grew more and more frustrated and angry over this situ - ation. Eventually, they demanded that **Equity** staff and the **BAAC** do something about it.

Critics of the actors' union have always claimed that **Equity** policies are high-handed and unreasonable and that staff sometimes takes arbitrary action which throws a theatre management into con - fusion and creates disaster. It should be noted here that **BAAC** began meeting with company managers in 1977, urging them to correct inequities and that after four years of such discussions the managers had still made little improvement in actors' working con - ditions or salaries. In November of 1981, **BAAC** called a meeting of company managers and artistic directors at the **Plumbers' Union Building** on Market Street. Members of **BAAC** told these representatives of the various theatres that they must make adjust - ments in their budgets soon to include better pay for actors, and that if they did not then some change in the waiver plan would be inevitable. This warning was met by angry retorts from some managers and cries of dismay from others. Many of the managers claimed that **Equity** was trying to shut them down. They said they simply couldn't operate with better pay for actors in their budgets.

But the rank and file **Equity** members and the members of **BAAC** believed that they had been patient long enough. Nobody wanted the theatres to close, and nobody believed they would. Actors simply wanted the managers to re-think and adjust their bud - gets and to include a little better pay for performers' services in their annual planning. It was apparent, however, that the managers were not going to do this until **Equity** forced them to it.

The Waiver House sub-committee of **BAAC** held several meetings to discuss strategy. A proposal to change the waiver rules in and around the Bay area was prepared and presented to the members of **Equity** at its semi-annual meeting on March 29, 1982. This motion read as follows:

> RESOLVED that the following proposal, approved and amended by the Western Advisory Board and the New York Council, be put to referendum among the AEA members in northern California and, if passed, immediately implemented in the area:
>
> "As of September, 1982, all theatre companies in the Bay area shall be eligible for Equity Waiver classification only if the company's total gross annual operating budget, regardless of the number of production facilities used by the company, is less than $100,000, the maximum seating capacity of each facility is 99, the rehearsal period of each play is no more than five consecutive weeks plus one week of previews, and the performance run of each play is no more than four perfor - mances per week for eight consecutive weeks. All AEA members performing under the waiver agreement must be iden - tified in the program by an asterisk referring to the statement: 'Appears through the courtesy of Actors' Equity Association.'"
>
> BE IT FURTHER RESOLVED that pro and con statements of no more than 150 words be included in the mailing when this proposal is put to referendum.
>
> Presented by
>
> Dean Goodman, Chairperson
> SF/BAAC Waiver House Committee

GENERAL MEMBERSHIP MEETING Monday, March 29, 1982

53

The discussion which followed the presentation of this motion clarified that this plan, if adopted 1) would not eliminate the waiver system but would simply redefine and limit it, 2) would not force any theatre company to use **Equity** actors at all if it did not wish to do so, 3) would not require any theatre with an annual budget of less than $100,000 to pay actor salaries but would indeed require those with budgets over $100,000 to come to some other agreement with the union if they wished to cast **Equity** performers, 4) would limit the rehearsal time and playing time of any given production. It was generally agreed that, since most theatres ran their shows for five or six weeks, if a show was held over for more than eight weeks it must be doing good business and making money, and accordingly some agreement should be reached for paying actors if the run was to continue.

Two days before the meeting to discuss this motion it was reported in the San Francisco *Chronicle* that the membership was meeting to vote on a motion to eliminate the waiver plan in the Bay area. This was an erroneous report. The membership had no desire to eliminate the waiver plan. The desire was only to limit the plan and to require certain theatres to begin including salaries for actors in their budgets if they wished to use **Equity** actors. Moreover, the passage of the motion as worded only meant that the proposal to limit the waiver would go to referendum—a mail vote—since any vote at a general membership meeting would not be inclusive of all actors who might wish to have a voice in the decision. (General business meetings are seldom attended by more than 10-15% of the entire membership, as is the case with most union meetings.) The misleading *Chronicle* report incited more paranoia concerning **Equity**, as the press often does, and it is an unfortunate example of how one or two careless journalists can influence public opinion in the wrong direction.

At any rate, the motion to limit the waiver plan in the Bay area did indeed go to referendum and it was passed by an overwhelming number of **Equity** actors living in the district.

Negotiations began immediately with the various theatres that had annual budgets of more than $100,000. These negotiations took several months and were aided by Judson Barteaux, head of Equity's **Developing Theatres Committee** in New York, who came to San Francisco to meet with **BAAC** and the individual managers. Barteaux devised a plan of using **Letters of Agree-**

54

ment and what he called **Policy Statements**, two arrangements which were intended to be stepping stones to more standard **Equity** contracts. The **LOA**s and **Policy Statements**, which differed with each theatre company, included some stipulations concerning rehearsals and working conditions and also specified rates of payment for actors. The idea was that these agreements were to be in effect for a three year period and that they would be periodically reviewed. Everybody hoped that these theatre managers would now begin consciously to build their companies into full **Equity** opera - tions.

That is precisely what happened. The managers who had them - selves resisted **BAAC**'s requests for years now accepted the man - date of the referendum and over a period of six to eight months began to implement the agreements which **Equity** had negotiated with them. None of these theatres were forced to close, as some managers had threatened they might or as others had feared they would if they "went **Equity**." Instead the calibre of their produc - tions and their prestige only increased. It is true that the **Berkeley Stage** in Berkeley shut down within a year or so but Angela Paton, its Artistic Director, was quick to declare that her theatre was beset with other problems and that its demise was not due to its agreement with **Equity** or any pressure from the union.

At this time another organization, **Bay Area Theatre Work - ers Association**, had been formed to aid non-union actors, direc - tors and technicians in their dealings with theatre managements. **BATWA** announced that it was sympathetic with **Equity**'s views and that both organizations could work towards similar ends, although some sense of rivalry between the two groups seemed apparent. It happened, however, that the **Equity LOA**s permitted many non-union people who had been members of **BATWA** to join **Equity** and a large number of them chose to do so, including people who had been **BATWA** leaders. All of this had nothing but a positive effect since, with the pool of local **Equity** actors grow - ing, managements almost had to deal with **Equity** in one way or another if they wanted to use the better local actors.

The **Eureka Theatre** was founded by Robert Woodruff and Chris Silva as the **Shorter Players** in 1972. For many years the groups' productions were staged in the **Trinity Methodist**

Church at 2299 Market Street, until a disastrous fire destroyed these premises and the company found a new home, for a time, in the old **Margaret Jenkins Dance Studio** at 15th and Mission Streets. Then fire code restrictions compelled the company to seek still other headquarters. An old warehouse was found at 2730 16th Street, a campaign was launched to raise funds to convert the space into a theatre with adjacent offices, scene shop and storage quarters, and the first **Eureka** production in this location was Caryl Chur - chill's *Top Girls,* which opened on January 16, 1985. The com - pany had previously scored a huge success with Churchill's *Cloud Nine*, which was moved from the **Jenkins** studio to the **Marines Memorial** and then the new **Alcazar** at 650 Geary Street, both theatres which could accommodate larger audiences.

The **Eureka Theatre** company was one of the groups which, during what **Equity** staff and members throughout the country came to call "The San Francisco Experiment," went from a waiver house status to a **Letter of Agreement** and is expected to proceed to the new **Small Professional Theatres** contract which **Equity** has implemented on a national basis. The **Eureka** is an excellent ex - ample of how a theatre company with modest beginnings but high artistic standards and good business acumen can develop into a full-scale professional **Equity** company.

A great deal of the credit for this development must rest with business manager Mary Mason and the artists who have remained loyal and dedicated to this group's ideas and ideals. Richard E. T. White and Alma Becker were two of the company's first prominent directors. White has now gone on to direct elsewhere, most notably in this area with the **Berkeley Shakespeare Company** and the **Berkeley Repertory**. Becker now works mainly in New York, but she returns to the Bay area occasionally to direct a production or teach and direct with the **Playwrights Festival** in Marin County. Julie Hebert, now with the **Magic Theatre**, also directed for the **Eureka** in its early days. The current Artistic Director Anthony Taccone, and stage directors Richard Seyd and Oskar Eustis have maintained and enhanced the first declared policy of the **Eureka**, which is to present "Bay area premieres of dynamic, contemporary plays which illuminate important social issues and avenues for social change." The **Eureka** has non-profit status and receives funding from several organizations. Apart from Taccone, Seyd and Eustis, Susan Marsden is a director who has worked consistently with this company over the past few seasons. Although auditions are open to all members of the theatre community, the company does have a nucleus of actors which it uses on a more or less regular basis. Among women, the better known of these include Sigrid Wur - schmidt, Lori Holt and Abigail Van Alyn. Male actors who often appear at the **Eureka** include Will Marchetti, Jack Shearer, Joseph Miksak, Morgan Upton and Julian Lopez-Morillas.

The **Magic Theatre** has been in existence for almost twenty years. It started in a bar in Berkeley, moved to space above another bar, the **Rose and Thistle** at California and Polk Streets in San Francisco, and finally found a more permanent home in the middle 70s in Building C at **Fort Mason Center**. The **Magic** now oper - ates two theatres at this location. John Lion is the founder of this company and remains the General Director. Although he functions as chief administrator, he also directs and occasionally acts at the **Magic**. Lion has always maintained that his theatre is essentially a playwrights' theatre and the **Magic** presents mostly new works by modern writers, with an occasional revival of a past success. Sev - eral of Sam Shepard's and Michael McClure's new plays have been tried out here before they have gone on to other productions else - where. Shepard's *True West* was especially successful, and after a profitable run at **Fort Mason** was moved to the **Marines Memo - rial** where it ran for several more weeks. The company has non-profit status and lists more than twenty organizations from which it receives funding as a supplement to its box-office receipts.

Like the **Eureka**, the **Magic** went from waiver house status to an Equity **Letter of Agreement** during the early negotiations of the San Francisco Experiment. However, in 1985 the production of a play called *The Couch* by Lynn Kaufman and featuring popular local actors Kenna Hunt and Jack Shearer was such a box-office hit that its run was extended with a raise in pay for the actors involved.

Since emphasis at the **Magic** is more on plays than players, this theatre has developed no clear nucleus of actors nor a particular style, although many actors who have worked at the **Magic** have gone on to national renown. These include John Vickery, Peter Coyote, Ed Harris and a few others. Will Marchetti, Sigrid Wur - schmidt and Drew Eshelman are among performers, now working elsewhere in and around San Francisco, who have appeared at the **Magic**. Directors such as Ted Shank and Simon Levy, who di -

rected *The Couch*, have been invited to return and to direct other productions.

A spokesperson for the theatre says, "The **Magic** is proud of all of its productions, even the ones that critically fail."

The **One Act Theatre Company** was formerly called the **Berkeley One Act Theatre Company**. It was founded in 1976 by Jean Schiffman, Peter Tripp and Lauralee Westaway. "Berkeley" was dropped from the company name when the group took over the old **Encore**, once operated by the **Actor's Workshop** and also as a home for independent productions, and it was later re-named **The Showcase**. The **One Act Theatre** moved into this space in 1977 and began to build a loyal following. Another non-profit organiza-tion, the **One Act Theatre** receives grants from several foun-dations, maintains a permanent staff and has a board of directors. As the name indicates, the **One Act** was founded chiefly for the pur-pose of producing short plays. As time went on, however, the reservoir of one act comedies or dramas which seemed suitable for production grew smaller and the need for new one acts became more apparent. Following the success of a play called *Sylvester the Cat vs. Galloping Billy Bronco* playwright Michael Lynch was ap-pointed Playwright-in-Residence, and for a time the company pro-duced several new works, both by Lynch and by gay playwright Daniel Curzon, in a theatre adjacent to the **One Act**'s main stage. Curzon's *Last Resort*, set in a gay bar, was particularly effective and his *Margaret and Ernie versus the World* featured Linda Powell and Gerald Winer, two of the company's most prominent character actors.

Peter Tripp was Artistic Director of the **One Act** into the 1980s. Then, as happens with many theatre groups, there was dis-agreement over policies and practices. Tripp resigned. His place was taken for a brief period by Ric Prindle. Prindle relinquished this post after a year or two and Simon Levy, previously a free-lance director, was appointed to replace him. Levy has continued with the policy of presenting short plays, but he has also expressed a desire to produce longer works. One of his first offerings was the 1985 San Francisco premiere of Arthur Miller's *Playing for Time*.

A unique part of the **One Act**'s schedule has been its Lunch-time Theatre, a program of short plays presented during the noon hour. These mid-day performances have met with popular approval and success, but were unfortunately discontinued in 1986.

Many local actors have gained recognition through appearances at the **One Act**. Jean Schiffman and Lauralee Westaway, two of the company's founders, continue to act from time to time. Mark Todd is a young leading man who has displayed his versatility in a num - ber of **One Act** productions. Priscilla Alden and Wanda McCad - den, non-union for a time, have subsequently become **Equity** mem - bers and work elsewhere as well as in the space at 430 Mason Street. Veterans Joseph Miksak and Kenna Hunt have also appeared here, as have Adele Proom, Irving Israel and Joe Bellan.

The **One Act** has operated under a **Policy Statement** since the beginning of the San Francisco Experiment, but is expected to work out some sort of sliding scale upgrading process with the union for actors' salaries. The management has expressed its desire to become a full **Equity** company within three to five years and in early 1986 began fundraising to finance an enlarged seating capacity for the theatre.

The **San Francisco Repertory Theatre**, founded in 1972 by Michelle Truffaut who is the current Artistic Director, was incor - porated in 1974 and began producing plays in the Castro area at 4147 19th Street near Collingwood in 1976. The company was under-financed and had a rough time of it for several seasons. Even - tually, however, better actors began to work at the **Rep** and the cali - bre of productions improved. Although the **Rep**'s annual budget fell below the $100,000 cut-off figure and the company could have con - tinued with its waiver status, Truffaut and her advisors chose to be - gin operation under a **Policy Statement** and so continued through 1985.

In late 1985 the **Rep** began renting its space for independent waiver productions such as the **Tale Spinners'** *Working* and *LBJ*, a production by the **Lorraine Hansberry Theatre**. Truffaut and her company went in search of a new home. A special arrange - ment was made with **Equity** whereby the capacity at the **Victoria Theatre,** on 16th Street near Mission, could be limited to 200 seats and the **Rep** could produce two plays there in the spring of 1986, using some union actors and some who were non-union. Truffaut and Michael Addison were set to direct. The **Rep** has built its repu - tation with the production of British and American plays which might be considered modern classics and with rarely-produced plays by middle Europeans. From all indications the company will con -

tinue with this policy, without a permanent nucleus of performers and casting most actors from open auditions.

These, then, were the waiver theatres in San Francisco that re - sponded to the **Equity** membership, entered into negotiations with the union staff and became part of the San Francisco Experiment to develop ninety-nine seat houses into more professional operations.

Though the proposal adopted by the **Equity** membership in 1982 did not eliminate the waiver plan in San Francisco, it did in - deed change the character of the waiver as it operates in this area.

Also, one or two companies which exceeded the $100,000 annual budget limitation and were therefore ineligible for the waiver under the new rules still wished to continue production. They elec - ted to operate as non-**Equity** companies, often with skilled per - formers but without the services of many of the better-known actors in the city.

In 1986 most of the managements which apply for the use of the waiver are independent producers who do not have an estab - lished company nor a permanent home. While some of them may develop into companies presenting a season of plays in an estab - lished space, only three of them—the **Asian-American Theatre, Theatre Rhinoceros**, and the **Lorraine Hansberry The - atre**—currently offer a regular schedule of plays. These are ethnic groups which will be discussed in more detail in a later chapter.

Perhaps the best known of the theatres which no longer has the waiver but chose not to go to a **Letter of Agreement** or **Policy Statement** with **Equity** is the **Julian Theatre** at 953 De Haro Street. The **Julian** does occasionally use an **Equity** member under a special **Guest Artist** contract, but its actors are mainly non-union performers. The **Julian** is one of the oldest theatre companies in San Francisco and was incorporated by Richard Reineccius together with Douglas Giebel in 1965. Eight to twelve productions are of - fered each season. The management states that plays chosen "must have social relevance or be new plays premiering in this area or in the world."

Funding for the **Julian** comes from the **National Endow - ment for the Arts**, the **California Arts Council**, the San Francisco Hotel Tax Fund, the **San Francisco Foundation**, the

Hewlett Foundation, the **Fleishhacker Foundation**, and the **Goethe Institute** as well as from box-office receipts.

Aided by the **California Arts Council**, the **Julian** has taken some of its productions on tour throughout the state. It has also imported full productions by various groups and has featured festivals of plays by new playwrights, a series specially funded. New acting, writing and technical talent is welcomed, and the company frequently offers classes and invites audience discussions. Several of the **Julian**'s productions have received awards from the **Bay Area Theatre Critics Circle**, Brenda Berlin's excellent 1980 production of *Getting Out* as one example.

The **Actors' Ark**, founded in 1971, was a company which served the community for slightly more than a decade. Martin Ponch, one of the founders of the **Interplayers**, was the Artistic Director of this group, and Ugo Baldassari was its Producing Director. The **Ark** had non-profit status and operated with some volunteer workers and some paid staff and performers. Significant but rarely-performed plays by both classical and contemporary writers were produced in various locations throughout the city. The company's demise, according to spokespersons, was due to an inability to find a permanent and suitable space in which to perform coupled with financial problems caused by the "wandering minstrel" syndrome. The final year of its existence the **Ark** did have a home in Building F at **Fort Mason Center**, but the company could not negotiate a lease for continued use of this space and Brecht's *Puntila and His Man Matti* in 1982 proved to be the **Ark**'s final offering to San Francisco theatregoers.

The **Actors' Ensemble** was another waiver company which operated for a time under the management of Philip Pruneau and then Stephanie Priest. Productions were staged in a basement space at 2940 16th Street during the 1970s and a wide variety of plays were produced. Many local actors appeared in **Ensemble** shows, including such well-known performers as Kenna Hunt, Roberta Callahan, Elizabeth Keller, Kirk Ullery and William Wilson. Keller and Wilson were leading players of Stephanie Priest's personal stock company, and when she left the **Ensemble** the two actors went with her to the **San Francisco Repertory** and the **Actors' Ark** where she directed other plays with these performers in leading roles.

61

The **Bedini Theatre Project** was founded in 1979 by Law - rence Bedini and staged productions for a time at 3368 Jackson Street, then 347 Dolores at 16th Street. A producing group known as **Nova** occupies the Dolores Street space in 1986.

During the 70s and early 80s there were, of course, many independent waiver productions staged in such spaces as the **Inter - section** near Washington Square, the **Zephyr** at 595 Mission Street, and the **People's Theatre Coalition** at **Fort Mason Center**, the latter facility used by the **Asian-American Theatre** in 1986. Now that Michelle Truffaut has moved her company into larger quarters, the **San Francisco Repertory** space on 19th Street and Collingwood is being used by such groups as the **Tale Spinners, Shoestring Productions** and the **Lorraine Hans - berry Theatre** for single productions. Other shows have been pre - sented at **Theatre Artaud** and **Studio Eremos** on Florida Street, and productions sponsored by the old **Intersection** are now pre - sented at the company's new location, the former **Valencia Rose**. All of these spaces will no doubt continue to be used for the next few years for single productions if not for groups producing on a regular schedule.

Entrepreneur Steve Dobbins, who has also been a director and playwright, is currently developing a complex at 25 Van Ness Avenue which will include three small theatres in the basement area plus larger spaces on the seventh floor. A new company called the **Chamber Theatre** opened the ninety-nine seat waiver space with a production of Pinter's *The Homecoming* in March of 1986. Michael Koppy presented his version of *March of the Falsettos* at 25 Van Ness Avenue, also in the spring of '86.

The members of **Equity**'s 1986-'87 **Bay Area Advisory Committee** believe that the waiver plan will continue in San Fran - cisco, with independent productions staged from time to time, but that most managers who wish to develop an ensemble group of performers will consider the waiver simply as the first step toward a full professional company under **Equity** contract.

5

THE COMMERCIAL INDEPENDENTS

There are occasional hardy souls who live in the Bay area or who, having heard that San Francisco is an exciting city with a keen interest in theatre, come here from other parts of the country to present an independent production at one of the houses available for rent to commercial managements.

In some cases, while these shows have been performed successfully and have made money in other cities, they may or may not do well in San Francisco. In other cases, a play or musical revue has never been staged elsewhere but the producer thinks it will be a smash hit in San Francisco. Maybe it will and maybe it won't. In either case, the producer has been able to beg, borrow or steal any - where from $30,000 to $150,000 from friends, relatives or profes - sional gamblers in order to get the show on the boards. (Funding organizations don't usually give grants to commercial managements, so backing for these kinds of presentations must come from indi - viduals.) Then the producer crosses his or her fingers and prays.

It's a risky business.

Very few of these productions enjoy a healthy run, and even those that manage to last for a few weeks or months seldom make any money. A large percentage, if they do not get good reviews, close within a couple of days or weeks. Even those that are well received by the press do not necessarily start doing good business right away. (These shows, remember, do not have the ready-made subscription audience that goes to **A.C.T.** or Carole Shorenstein's series.) Many plays or musicals linger on and play for six months or a year, which is wonderful for the performers who are working steadily and collecting their salaries. It is not always so wonderful for the producers. While a show keeps running and is established in the public's mind as a success, it is often just meeting operating ex - penses from week to week and may have paid back very little of the original production costs. Many shows close with the backers' in - vestments totally down the drain.

Talks with some of these independent producers, and with press agents and company managers who are sophisticated and who know the problems involved with commercial producing in San Francisco, reveal interesting and significant pieces of information.

Tom Parlett is a company manager who, over the past decade, has handled the business details at such theatres as the new **Alca - zar**, the **Little Fox**, the **On Broadway**, the **Curran** and **The - atre-On-The-Square.** A company manager, perhaps it should be explained, is a person who minds the store for the producer, keeps his books, makes up the payroll, deals with union details and dis - putes, supervises the box-office and house personnel, soothes upset performers and technicians and, in general, takes care of the day-to-day problems and emergencies.

When I questioned Parlett concerning his views and opinions, we started reminiscing and tried to recall a few of the productions he has managed since he first came to the Bay area in 1975. We came up with a long list of titles, not including a stint he did with the Ice Follies. The very number of jobs he has held over the past decade is itself an indication of how short-lived some of the runs were. Yet several of these productions were touring shows with national repu - tations—such "hits" as *Eubie, For Colored Girls Who Have Considered Suicide, A . . . my name is Alice* and the Rex Harrison-Claudette Colbert starrer *Aren't We All?* Others were shows that got good notices and were considered successes here, including Dick Shawn's *The Second Greatest Entertainer in the World, Snoopy, The Mousetrap, All Night Strut, The Passion of Dracula, Betty Garrett and Other Songs* and *Bleacher Bums,* among others.

64

"I've been lucky," says Parlett. "I've worked with, and for, some of the best."

Is there a formula for success as an independent producer in today's San Francisco?

"In the commercial theatre," says Parlett, "sad to say, serious plays don't make it here. The public wants musicals and revues, or far-out zany farces. A star name helps. You have to remember, a show at the **Alcazar**, the **Marines Memorial** or **Theatre-On-The-Square** is competing with the touring shows at the **Geary** and the **Curran**."

Well, what about favorable reviews? Do they help a show to become successful at the box-office?

"They're no guarantee of success. A bad review will kill busi - ness, that's for sure, but a good review won't necessarily make a show a hit, at least not right away. A producer has to have good le - gal and accounting advice, he has to understand marketing proce - dures and the importance of advertising before he decides to produce here. And, above all, he has to have enough financing to keep a show going for a few weeks until it catches on. Even with good reviews, a show has to run five or six weeks for the word of mouth to get around and for the box-office to start doing brisk business. A shorter run doesn't give the product a chance here.

"The major reviews are forgotten a day or two after they appear. But the summary mini-review which appears in the Sunday pink section of the *Examiner-Chronicle* every week, and the posi - tion of the little man in the sketch beside it is very important. The tourists who come to town probably haven't read the original review, but if they see that little man clapping or jumping out of his seat with enthusiasm they'll probably buy tickets to see the pro - duction. If the little man is slumped or has left his chair altogether, you might as well forget it. You won't attract the tourist trade, in that case, or the audience from suburbia, and without this sup - port—well, you might just as well strike the set and close the box-office."

Rudy Golyn, with his partner Lee Sankowich, produced sev - eral shows in San Francisco during the 1970s. These plays included *One Flew Over the Cuckoo's Nest*, which ran for five years at the **Little Fox Theatre** in North Beach, *The Mousetrap*, which ran for six months at the new **Alcazar**, and a couple of others which were somewhat less successful.

65

"The hard thing," said Golyn when I interviewed him, "is to find the right play to do in San Francisco. Lee and I both prefer shows with something meaningful to say, and we were lucky with *Cuckoo's Nest*. But you can't get away from it, what audiences are looking for here is sheer entertainment. A play that has too much depth isn't going to make it in commercial production in San Fran - cisco."

Golyn agrees with Tom Parlett that the position of the little man in the pink section of the Sunday paper is crucial to the success of an independent production on the local scene. (This cartoon character, perhaps it should be explained, is a kind of rating system for the quality of a production which has only an attached mini-review. If the little man is applauding and jumping out of his seat, this means that the show is a must-see. If he's sitting up and applauding, the message is conveyed that the production is above average. If he's sitting up but not applauding, he's telling readers that it's only so-so. If the little man is slumped in his seat or has left it altogether, he wants us to know that the show is a bomb.) "A plug from Herb Caen won't hurt your business, either," Golyn admits. *Cuckoo's Nest* was ready to close early in its run, because its initial reviews were not all that favorable. But an item in Caen's column in the *Chronicle* praised the show and gave it new life.

Even with help from the little man, however, a show has to hang on for quite a while to make back its initial investment and earn a profit. "The tourist trade is mainly in the summer," Golyn opines. "So what you have to produce here is a show which appeals not only to San Franciscans but to the suburbanites. You have to get them into town from Marin County and Walnut Creek if you want to break even and make a little money."

Golyn and Sankowich worked very closely together as they made their production plans. They both helped to raise the financ - ing, and they were both involved with selecting the cast and person - nel. Then, when it was time to start rehearsals, says Golyn, Sanko - wich took over as director and Golyn became the producer, handling the business affairs. The partners' last production here was *Bleacher Bums*, which opened as a waiver production at the **Zephyr The - atre** in the late 70s and then moved to an **Equity** contract produc - tion at the **Little Fox**. Neither of them has been active on the local theatre scene since that time.

66

The location of a theatre, or even the type of theatre into which a production is booked, may be a telling point in whether or not the show becomes a financial success.

A man named Esquire Jauchem was General Director of the **Boston Repertory Theatre** for several years in the early 70s. One of his most successful productions was an adaptation of Antoine de Saint-Exupéry's *The Little Prince*, which ran in Boston for five years. He raised the money for a production of this play in San Francisco, where he thought it would find a ready audience.

Jauchem's friends and advisors scouted the various sites in the city and decided that the best house in which to present this pro - duction, considering all factors, was the **Victoria Theatre** on 16th Street near Mission.

The **Victoria** is one of San Francisco's landmark theatres. Known as **Brown's Opera House**, it was a popular showcase for variety acts and vaudeville entertainers in the early part of this century. Then it became a burlesque theatre. The master lease was taken over in the late 70s by Robert and Anita Correa, who estab - lished what they called the **Theatre Guild of San Francisco**, under which name they presented such diversified productions as Brecht's *Mother Courage* and the famed dramatization of Erskine Caldwell's *Tobacco Road*. After a time, however, the Correas began to rent the **Victoria** out to independent groups such as the **San Francisco Mime Troupe,** various dance companies and gay the - atre productions. For a long time theatre workers had had their eyes on the **Victoria** as a middle-sized house which was ideal for certain kinds of productions, shows which were modestly budgeted but which required a capacity of more than ninety-nine seats. There seemed to be only one problem concerning the use of the **Victoria**: its location. Easily reached by public transportation, it is neverthe - less situated in what is not considered the "best" part of town. Would older people and the more affluent theatregoers be willing to patronize productions at the **Victoria**? Many producers and in - vestors thought not. For this reason, the Correas continued to rent to the odd choral group or dance company that wanted performing space for a weekend or a one-night appearance. More experienced entrepreneurs were wary of booking their shows into the **Victoria**.

Esquire Jauchem, however, decided to take a chance on the **Victoria** with his production of *The Little Prince*. Several people suggested to him that, with **Theatre Rhinoceros** operating across the street from the **Victoria** and with the **Eureka Theatre** doing well in its new location south of Market, perhaps the public attitude toward the area was changing. Maybe more theatregoers now wouldn't consider it quite so dangerous to travel to the Mission dis - trict to see a show, especially if it were a good production decidedly worth attending.

From a professional point of view, it seemed that Jauchem did everything right. To begin with, he had a property which was al - ready a proven success. He raised backing for his show which was said to be close to $150,000, certainly adequate financing for a mod - est production in a medium-sized theatre. He hired the same director who had staged the Boston production, and the same light and set designers. A top-notch, experienced stage manager, Michael Foley, was put on the payroll. From among local actors Jauchem and his director, David Zucker, selected a group of talented performers for the supporting roles, and for something of a name attraction they offered a key role to film actor John Phillip Law. As publicist, Jauchem contracted Violet Welles, a woman whose previous ac - counts had included *La Cage aux folles* and *My One and Only* at the **Golden Gate Theatre**. Bob Gunderson was hired as com - pany business manager and proper box-office help was employed. The entire staff, cast and crew would have been hard to beat on the San Francisco level.

The advertising budget for *The Little Prince* was extensive. Large ads appeared daily in the major press, ads which were in fact larger (and perhaps more attention-getting) than ads placed by many other local attractions. Radio and television spots were used, thou - sands of posters and flyers were distributed. Balloons were blown up and let fly on major streets. It would have been hard for anyone living in San Francisco who could read or who listened to the radio or watched television not to know that a production of *The Little Prince* was opening at the **Victoria Theatre**.

In addition to all of this, a substantial amount of money was spent in sprucing up the theatre itself. The entire lobby was painted and redesigned and decorated with plants and floral displays. A huge banner with the play's title was flown above the marquee; the old marquee lettering was changed to brilliant red to attract attention of people who passed by. Inside the theatre, the seats were cleaned and vacuumed. Cracks in the walls and ceiling were repaired and painted. The proscenium arch of the stage itself was redesigned.

This work was done at the expense of Jauchem's production company, not the theatre management.

During previews the producer was generous in giving com-
plimentary tickets to theatre people and others who might spread
good word about the production. Opening night festivities were handled with style, in a fashion not often seen in San Francisco. Klieg
lights were in front of the theatre, celebrities arrived in limousines.
An opening night party was held in the **Hall of Flowers** in
Golden Gate Park, a party replete with food and drink and a rock
band for dancing. Spirits were high, since the reaction to the production overall so far had been good.

When the reviews appeared in the major press they were not
unfavorable. In general they praised the direction and the supporting
cast. The only controversy was over the performance of Hollywood
actor John Phillip Law, called "wooden" by Bernard Weiner in his
Chronicle review. But there was no little man jumping out of his
seat beside the mini-review in the Sunday paper.

In a panic, the producer and his backers decided to replace Law
with director David Zucker who had been greatly praised in the Boston production. Weiner was invited to review the show again, which
he did, and he seemed more favorably impressed with Zucker's performance than he had been with Law's. But while business continued to be fairly good, there was no sudden increase of activity at the
box-office. In fact, weekly income was not meeting the operating
costs.

Jauchem was in a quandary as to what to do. He had initially
advertised a six-week run to end on December 29th, but had really
believed (due to the show's great success in Boston) that an extension of the San Francisco run was almost a foregone conclusion. He
worked out a deal with the Correas and with **Equity** to continue the
run with reduced rent on the theatre and under a different union contract whereby the actors would perform fewer shows at a smaller
weekly salary. All were anxious to cooperate with him, since everybody believed that, in general, public reaction to the production had
been good and there was still life in it.

Then, suddenly, after good holiday business, there was no advance sale for the month of January. Jauchem met with his investors
and they decided to close the show. The entire original investment
had been lost.

I talked with Jauchem about a month after *The Little Prince* closed. Although saddened by his San Francisco experience, he was not totally discouraged. He still has faith in *The Little Prince* and plans to present it elsewhere in the country. He thinks San Francisco is a tough theatre town, from a producer's stand - point, but he is not averse to reviving his show here if he can find a smaller theatre which is more suitable for an intimate production. He is convinced that while *The Little Prince* did somewhat change the image of the **Victoria**, and while many people who had previously been unwilling to travel into the Mission district to see a show in an old burlesque house did take that risk, many other potential custom - ers stayed away because of the alleged "unsafe" area in which the theatre is located. Also, like many producers, he thinks perhaps his show didn't get a completely fair shake from the reviewers. But he may very well present *The Little Prince* in San Francisco again. "It's a charming show," he said. "A lot of people who still haven't seen it would enjoy it, I'm sure."

Roberta Bleiweiss, a well-known publicist in the area, agrees with others when she says the location or type of theatre into which a show is booked may be a telling point in whether or not the show is a financial success.

"I met Jim Freyburg when he produced a musical revue called *Starting Here, Starting Now* at the **Little Fox** a few years ago," she says. "It was a delightful show, but it didn't make it here because it was presented in the wrong atmosphere. An intimate little show like that didn't belong in a theatre. It should have been per - formed in a cabaret setting. If it had been packaged properly and played in the right surroundings, I think it might have enjoyed a better run."

Bleiweiss says that an independent producer who wants to pre - sent a show in San Francisco should know the city and should know what San Franciscans like. "The public here goes for proven material or it likes to discover something, a show that's new and unusual. If it's a bit on the freaky side, so much the better."

This is a lady who should know what she's talking about, because she and her sister Nancy were among the creators of the original *Beach Blanket Babylon*, a show that was far out and campy enough to delight audiences as well as critics from the beginning.

"When Jim Freyburg called to tell me that he wanted to bring a show called *The Asparagus Valley Cultural Society* to the Bay

70

area," Bleiweiss continues, "I told him he had ten points in his favor right away. San Franciscans respond to a title like that."

The show lived up to its freaky title and the public did respond to it, apparently, because *Asparagus Valley*, an entertainment in which three young men engaged in zany musical bits, comedy routines and magic acts ran three years at the **Phoenix Theatre** on Broadway in North Beach.

According to Freyburg, however, this production didn't become a success overnight. The producer claims that his show was in the red for the first six months of its run. If true, this substantiates the opinions of Tom Parlett, Rudy Golyn and many others whom I have interviewed that even a fine production will often take a while to find its audience, recoup its investment and earn a profit. The pro-ducer who is anxious to present a play or a revue in San Francisco, therefore, must have substantial backing and must be prepared to operate at a loss for some time before the production works its way into the black. There is no real guarantee, either, that it will ever do that. It's all a crap shoot.

Jonathan Reinis, alone or in partnership with others, has pro-duced a number of professional shows in San Francisco, including *How the Other Half Loves* and Eve Merriam's *The Club* at the **On Broadway**, *Shay Duffin as Brendan Behan* and *Tom Taylor as Woody Guthrie* at the **Cannery Theatre**, and Peter Donat in *Spaghetti in Tugboats* at the **Little Fox**. With his partner Joseph Perrotti, Reinis now holds the lease on **Theatre-On-The-Square**, a former Elks Club auditorium on Post Street near Powell. Reinis and Perrotti opened **Theatre-On-The-Square** with a production of Lanford Wilson's *Talley's Folly*, which was a considerable suc-cess. They have booked touring productions of such hit shows as *Mass Appeal* and *Torch Song Trilogy*, but this new theatre space has also housed some resounding failures, late 1985's *Roller Der-by* being one of them. *A . . . my name is Alice*, which had been a big success in New York, did not do as well here as expected.

Reinis, who admits he has trouble finding good shows either to produce himself or book into **Theatre-On-The-Square**, paints a bleak picture for the producer of independent shows in San Fran-cisco.

"In San Francisco," he explains, "due to increased theatre rental charges, higher advertising costs, plus union demands for ac-tors and technicians, the expense of mounting a show has more than

71

doubled over the past few years. Ticket prices are high, but they have not gone up commensurately with production costs. Chances are very slim indeed for recouping the original cost of a new show mounted in the Bay area. No new plays produced here have ever, to my knowledge, been picked up for commercial film or television, so there's no chance of a profit from the sale of subsidiary rights, as there is from a play done on Broadway in New York."

Still, Reinis says, the Bay area is his home and he has an affec-tion for San Francisco. He does believe that there is an audience for good independently-produced shows here. He doesn't want to leave town. But if he is ever forced to do so, it will be the reluctant deci-sion of a man who has been considered a success as a local pro-ducer.

From time to time independent productions have been tried out in an **Equity** waiver house situation. A few of these have been suc-cessful enough for the producer to move them into larger theatres under full union contracts. The **Eureka Theatre** production of *When You Comin' Back, Red Ryder?* which moved into the **Little Fox** in the mid-70s is an example of such a case, as was the Sanko-wich-Golyn production of Arthur Kopit's *Indians* which went from a store-front to the **Montgomery Playhouse** on Broadway. (The **Montgomery**, not previously mentioned in this text, was a theatre space leased and managed for a time by Jane Montgomery. Before her tenancy the house gained fame as the home of **The Com-mittee**, perhaps the most noted of all improvisational groups which have performed in the city. Under Jane Montgomery's management the house was host to a dozen or so different comedies and dramas during the 70s.) In the fall of 1979 Jonathan Reinis moved his pro-duction of *How the Other Half Loves* from **The Showcase** at 430 Mason Street (now known as the **One Act Theatre**) where it had done excellent business to the **On Broadway**. None of these shows which had been successful in small theatres, however, re-peated or continued their successes in larger houses. The Sanko-wich-Golyn production of *Bleacher Bums*, which moved from a waiver production at the **Zephyr** to the **Little Fox** in the summer of 1981, closed very shortly after its transfer.

When one has talked with a great many producers of local independent shows and gathered many opinions, and when one has been a long-time observer of the San Francisco theatre scene, a curious dilemma becomes apparent: how is it possible, when the ap-

72

proval of both press and public is necessary for a show to be a financial success, and when the tastes of press and public are often dissimilar, to please both of these factions at the same time? Favorable reviews are absolutely essential to get a show off the ground commercially, but what happens when the play is excellent within its genre but does not happen to be the kind of play which is particularly liked by the *Chronicle* reviewer, for example?

Evidence shows that the public responds to escapist entertain - ment, or more conventional style comedies and dramas. Yet the major critics in San Francisco at the present time are not particularly receptive to so-called formula entertainment and, in general, react more favorably to esoteric, avant-garde works. This predilection on the part of the critics influences, in some people's opinion, the types of plays which a producer chooses to present here (because the pro - ducer needs that little man jumping out of his chair for his show to be a financial success). The question arises as to whether or not this is a healthy situation. While the argument can always be made that one of a critic's functions is to try to raise the taste of the general public, is the theatre meant only for elitist intellectuals and must every theatregoer's taste be similar to that of a given critic's?

Ruby Cohn is a respected professor of dramatic literature at the **University of California at Davis**. In the February 9, 1986 edition of the *Chronicle* she reviewed a book by the late Alan Schneider, a well-known American director. In reference to Schnei - der's most commercially successful production, a play by Robert Anderson called *You Know I Can't Hear You When the Water's Running*, she stated that Schneider "is under no illusion that any discerning reader will want to hear about that slick entertainment."

I knew Alan Schneider personally, and while he may have been prouder of his productions of Albee's *The Zoo Story* and *Who's Afraid of Virginia Woolf?* than he was of many of his other works, I cannot believe that he didn't recognize the place which plays like that of Anderson's rightfully have in the American theatre.

"This condescension in Cohn's tone," one producer said to me, "is typical of the attitude which many of our critics have today. A kind of inverted snobbism exists among the current San Francisco critics. This makes a producer think not whether he likes and wants to produce a certain play, or whether he thinks the public will like it. He has to think whether it's the kind of play Bernard Weiner of the *Chronicle* will approve, because he needs a favorable review from the *Chronicle* in order to succeed with his show. The question is, ought we to produce in San Francisco only the kinds of plays or musicals which appeal to the tastes of one man and his followers, or should we produce plays which appeal to all tastes? Which is fairer and more reasonable?"

(A later section in this book will deal with the critics in more detail. It might be appropriate at this point, however, to quote a local actor on how he thinks the critics have also affected acting styles in this area. "Everybody knows how Weiner likes off-the-wall plays," says this well-known performer who, for obvious reasons, asked not to be identified. "He also seems to have a thing for insecure performances. A smooth, polished performance he is likely to label mannered or superficial, but he will often give his best review to an actor whose work is unfocused or faltering. A few years ago I was in a play with a man whose performance Weiner called brilliantly naturalistic. This notice was a source of great amusement to the other actors in the show, because we all knew that what Weiner called rich nuance was merely the struggle of the poor actor to remember his lines. What model was Weiner holding up for the rest of us to emulate? Even the actor who got the rave review from Weiner was embarrassed by the critical acclaim. He knew he didn't deserve it.")

In his excellent book *Journey to the Center of the Theatre* (Knopf, 1979) Walter Kerr talks about the effect, both good and bad, of the avant-garde on American playwriting. The theatre, he says, has lost something because of this movement. Writers. In Kerr's opinion we may have lost an entire generation of potential dramatists (not to mention actors who have been trained to speak the words of such dramatists) because of the vogue for the avant-garde and the neglect of the conventional, realistic form. A playwright who writes a realistic play today has little chance, or at least far less chance than the avant-garde writer, of getting his play produced. So, Kerr concludes, we may take profit from what has gone on, but all that has gone on has left many a potential dramatist crippled. Theatregoers, too, we might infer, have been and are being deprived. A product which might please many of us can find no market.

Breaking the formula, of course, isn't easy, either. *Beach Blanket Babylon* and all of its subsequent variations on the original theme managed to do it. Ron House, Diz White and Allen Sherman did it for a while with their **Low Moan Spectacular Company**

74

and their long-running productions of *El Grande de Coca Cola* and *Bullshot Crummond* at the **Hippodrome Theatre**, but their last effort, *Footlight Frenzy*, ran only a few months at the **Alcazar** and wasn't a comparable hit.

One of the mistakes which the producing team of John Anto-nelli and Rita Abrams may have made when they produced a play with music called *Pink Moon* at the **Old Venetian Bakery** near Bay and Powell Streets in late 1980 was to assume that since San Francisco is the so-called gay capital of the world, any play with a homosexual or bisexual theme will be supported by the gay com-munity here. Not so. Gay theatregoers are just as discriminating, and often just as prejudiced, as straight theatregoers. Gay people will not attend a play in large numbers simply because it is suppo-sedly oriented to their life style; they have to be assured that it is a good play first. Also, the gay community is split into many factions, some liberal and some conservative. The gay men who spend their lives on Castro Street will not necessarily identify with a play about two elegant gay men who share an apartment and an affluent life style in Pacific Heights, and vice versa. What is interesting and pro-vocative to one gay man or lesbian will not appeal to another, just as what appeals to one straight person does not necessarily appeal to another.

Abrams, an Emmy award-winning composer, and her friend John Antonelli, a television and film producer, nevertheless thought they had a winner with *Pink Moon*, a play about an upfront gay man and his relationship with a kooky neighbor girl and their rivalry for the affections of a young male bisexual. The show was a sort of gay *They're Playing Our Song*, with a soft rock score by Abrams. They raised the necessary backing, hired experienced singer-actors, con-structed an attractive set, employed professional musicians for the pit and opened *Pink Moon* late in 1980.

"Audiences, and some critics," Abrams told me, "did love the show. But the major press was ruthless with us, to our shock, cha-grin and anger. We expected support, or at least fairness, but instead received aloof and highbrow treatment, with no acknowledgment of the positive audience response. I will never understand the angry tone of those all-powerful reviews. It was as if we were trying to commit a crime rather than entertain."

Despite the somewhat resentful tone of this statement, Rita Abrams is a warm and appealing young woman who does not project undue hostility but conveys instead an impression that she has a sincere concern for the state of San Francisco theatre. "Besides lowering my expectations," she says, "the only thing I would do next time would be to open somewhere other than San Francisco. The *Chronicle* theatre section has a stronghold on criticism unlike any other major city paper." (Since *Pink Moon* in 1980 Antonelli-Abrams have presented no other shows in San Francisco.)

A study of so-called gay plays presented here over the years is further evidence that the gay community does not necessarily dis - regard reviews and make a show a hit simply because it has a gay theme. The gay community did not rally around to save *Pink Moon*. *The Boys in the Band* and *Fortune and Men's Eyes* had only modest runs here in commercial productions, as did a show called *Tubstrip*. *P.S. Your Cat Is Dead* did fairly well at the **Mont - gomery** and, of course, the touring production of *Torch Song Trilogy* was a big success at **Theatre-On-The-Square**, but these shows came to town as New York hits with advance ballyhoo and they also received good local reviews. A locally produced gay play called *Special Friends* had mixed reviews when it was presented at **The Showcase** in the summer of 1975 but it did sell-out business for five weeks, probably because of a publicity campaign which promoted its attractive leading man to the gay community. When *Special Friends* was revived six years later at a theatre on Mission Street it did only moderate business. *Norman, Is That You?* played for months at the **On Broadway**, but there is some doubt as to whether this could be considered a gay play. It had a gay character, but in the main it was family oriented; it was written for straight audiences and it was not particularly supported by the gay com - munity. *Rusty*, the only original play by a local playwright ever to have a full **Equity** production here, was presented at the **Chi Chi** on Broadway in 1976. It developed a small cult following but closed after a five week run, its total investment lost.

Victor Wilmes' production of *The Club*, presented here by Reinis-Krempetz with an all-female cast dressed as men, did good business for a few months at the **On Broadway** in 1980. This may not have been strictly a gay play, either, but its success prompted Wilmes to bring another openly lesbian play called *Leap of Faith* here in the spring of 1981. He booked it into the **Old Vene - tian Bakery**, the same ninety-nine seat house where Antonelli-Abrams presented *Pink Moon*.

A resident of Phoenix, Wilmes loves San Francisco, he told me. "There's so much theatre going on here," he said. "It seems as if culture took an acid trip in the 60s and the theatre did, too. You can find an audience for anything you want to do here. It's easy to find the things you need for a production. The local unions are more cooperative, you get more help from the technical people—it's just great!"

This enthusiastic appraisal was made very early in the run of *Leap of Faith*. While the press and public appreciated the show's production values, the direction and the acting, the play itself was a short, fairly routine "coming-out" story and it never really caught the fancy of local theatregoers, straight or gay. *Leap of Faith* closed, at a considerable financial loss, after a two month run. Victor Wilmes was not available for comment, and despite his enthusiasm for San Francisco as a theatre town he has presented no other productions here since that time.

More attention will be given to gay theatre later in this text, but I have cited this information here to suggest that potential producers of plays with gay themes who think that such plays will be certain financial successes in San Francisco might do well to pause and think again.

Among the many theatre people with whom I talked as I worked on this chapter, perhaps the most optimistic concerning the present state of San Francisco theatre as well as its future, was a man named Charles Duggan. Duggan took a fifteen year lease on the **Marines Memorial Theatre** in July, 1982 and at the time I interviewed him in February, 1986 he had himself produced or booked eighteen different shows into the **Marines** over that two and one-half year period.

Duggan's record of successes is remarkably good. The **Eureka Theatre**'s production of *Cloud Nine* played the **Marines** for nine weeks before it moved to the **Alcazar**. *Greater Tuna*, a phenomenal success on the local scene, played the **Marines** for eleven weeks in early 1984, came back for eight weeks, and then went on to the **Alcazar** and eventually the **Mason Street Theatre** for continued good receptions. *A Soldier's Play*, *Corridos*, *Chinese Magic Circus*, *Jeeves Takes Charge*, *The American Dance Machine* and Charles Pierce in *An Intimate Extravaganza* were all productions which did well in Duggan's theatre.

77

"The very first production which I booked into the **Marines** was a dismal failure," said Duggan. "It was called *Pika*. I read the script and when the producers told me they had David McCallum for the leading role I thought the show had a good chance for success. I was wrong. *Pika* closed after only five performances."

Another disappointment to Duggan was the **Oregon Shake - speare Festival**'s production of *The Taming of the Shrew*, which did sell-out business for a trial run in Palo Alto but only lasted two weeks at the **Marines**, suffering a financial loss. "Perhaps people who like outdoor Shakespeare will go to Ashland for it, but when an Ashland production comes here and plays in a regular theatre the ambience isn't as attractive to them. Who knows?"

Duggan believes that a star name definitely helps at the box-office. His biggest success was *Sister Mary Ignatius Explains It All for You* which ran for twenty weeks in 1984, first with Lynn Redgrave and then with Cloris Leachman in the leading role. He grossed well over a million dollars with this attraction in his six hundred seat theatre. Other shows grossed a larger weekly average but did not play as long.

I asked the producer why he thought that *Greater Tuna*, which played two engagements at the **Marines**, had a long run at the **Alcazar** and then moved to the **Mason Street Theatre**, was so successful. "It isn't a cult show," he said, "although we had a lot of repeat business with it. It has a very wide appeal, amusing to a broad spectrum of the theatregoing public. The man on the street enjoys it as much as the intellectuals."

The money which Duggan has spent on productions which didn't succeed he considers an investment rather than a loss. He is sometimes frustrated, but he's not discouraged. He and his associ - ates keep faith with their audience, he told me; they are discriminat - ing about the packages they bring into the **Marines** and the shows they produce themselves. Two hundred thousand dollars has just been put into a renovation of the theatre. For the first time in sixty years the **Marines** has new seats, new lighting equipment and a re-designed proscenium opening to the stage. "Now we can plan ahead," says Duggan. "We can build a corporate audience and deal with conventions. We're trying to build a reputation for our theatre itself. We want people to say if it's at the **Marines** it must be okay."

78

Some theatre pieces, primarily those of a musical variety, have been presented in cabaret settings in San Francisco over the past several years. Though the initial production costs are usually far less, due to simpler staging and other factors, such shows face many of the same basic problems as those that open in regular theatres.

Ken Vega is a young composer-lyricist-director whose produc - tions of *There Was a Little Girl* and *Berlin '32* achieved recogni - tion and acclaim. His original musical *Marco Polo*, produced a bit more lavishly than the other two shows, opened at the **Savoy Tivoli** in North Beach in the early summer of 1981 but did not fare so well.

Speaking of *Berlin '32*, which played an irregular schedule at the **Chez Jacques**, California and Hyde Streets (a cabaret no lon - ger in operation) Vega says, "The show was produced on a real shoestring. Even so, it took eight months to get the original invest - ment back. It was a cooperative venture and performers were paid a percentage. We made a small profit during the last four months of the run. So nobody really got rich. But I think the cabaret setting is good for the modest tryout of an intimate musical show."

Perhaps the most successful of all cabaret shows in the city has been *Champagne! in a cardboard cup*, which played the **Chez Jacques** during its first year, then moved to the **Plush Room** of the **Hotel York** on Sutter Street, and also performed on the road. This show was totally financed by its producer-director, Kirk Frederick. "The budget for our show was very small," he says, "in line with the physical limitations of the space in which we opened. It took a year for me to get my money back. We were lucky, though—we had Noel Coward's music and later Cole Porter's fa - miliar melodies, tried and true material which we knew would please audiences, so we didn't have to win the critics' favor with new songs and lyrics. Also, we had a fine musical director, Doug Trantham, three excellent performers in Scott Rankine, Lynn Eldredge and Richard Roemer, and a splendid connective narrative arranged by Bill Gundel. The press was very good to us from the start. Still, while good reviews will sustain a show, they won't fill the house at every performance. You have to maintain an advertising campaign and never let up with your publicity."

Frederick, who has an office that does graphics and handles advertising for many other shows in town, noted that through his

79

business connections he has had access to many advertising chan -
nels that perhaps other producers do not. He has been able, for
example, to buy the front cover of *Key Magazine* on several occa -
sions. *Key* is a weekly tourist guide to entertainment and is widely
distributed in the city. Competition for its cover is very keen among
theatrical managements and the space must be reserved as long as a
year in advance. Sometimes, however, after reserving a cover, a
management will close its show and the space becomes available to
others.

"Whenever we've had a photo on the cover of *Key*," says
Frederick, "our business has doubled for the weekend."

Kirk Frederick warns that, especially during its early period, a
show must keep a cash reserve to balance slumps at the box-office.
Certain periods of the year are weak. July, for example is a weak
month. "Our business on Memorial Day and July 4th weekends with
Champagne was deadly. Business is also slow in January and
February, around tax time. You have to draw on your reserve, your
savings, to keep going during these bleak periods. Even a show that
has good reviews and which everybody considers to be a winner
doesn't have smooth sailing all the time."

Are there particular problems conected with doing a show in a
cabaret which are different from performing in a traditional theatre
setting?

"For one thing, there aren't that many cabarets in town where
you can stage a show. In 1986 the **Plush Room** or the **1177
Club** are about the only spaces available. But you don't usually
have to pay rent in a cabaret, that's an advantage, because the owner
makes his money from the drinks he sells and the show management
gets the door receipts, or at least a large share of them. The show
also has to be shorter than the usual musical in a theatre, no longer
than an hour and a half. The reason for that is, the owner often
books in another act following yours, at a later hour. That's an ad -
vantage or a disadvantage, depending on how you look at it. You
have to keep the show moving, too. There can't be throwaway num -
bers. People are drinking, remember, and you have to make them
pay attention to what's going on. In an intimate setting like a
cabaret, too, you have to exercise more care in maintaining your
costumes. The cleaning and pressing bills are probably larger for a
show in a cabaret than in a theatre."

Frederick's group, incorporated under the name of **Cameo Productions**, put the profits from *Champagne! in a cardboard cup* back into the company and used it to finance other productions. *By George*, a revue of songs by George Gershwin, was a moderate success but did not enjoy the same popularity as *Champagne*. In late 1985 Frederick presented *Thou Swell*, a tribute to Rodgers and Hart, at the **Mason Street Theatre**. This show received unfavor - able reviews and closed within a few days.

In the season 1985-'86 the only musical revue in a cabaret to achieve popular and critical acclaim was *Tune the Grand Up*, a pot - pourri of melodies by Jerry Herman, presented at the **1177 Club** on California Street.

With the exception of John Stark's notice in the *Examiner*, a show called *Dance Between the Lines*, presented at the **Music Hall Theatre** on Larkin Street near Geary, received nothing but rave reviews from the local critics. Even so, a conversation with producer-director Ann Marie Garvin reveals that, while considered a smash hit by the press and public when it opened in 1981, this oper - ation had many more problems and difficulties than most people realize.

Admittedly, many problems existed because of the unique nature of Garvin's project. I had heard, for example, that Garvin didn't merely rent the **Music Hall**, a former art house and gay disco, but that she bought the place, planning a long term tenancy.

"Well, the bank really owns it," she says with a shrug. "I still have to pay off the mortgage. But yes, you can say I bought the place. San Francisco is my home. My mother was a dancer on the old Fanchon and Marco vaudeville circuit and I used to dance at **Bimbo's**. I wanted to create a place where local dancers could work. I wanted to give talent here a chance to perform and to learn related theatre skills."

All of Garvin's staff members had multiple duties during the run of *Dance Between the Lines*. A multi-media show, the perfor - mance required the dancers to run the lights and sound in addition to their onstage duties. They also tended bar and served customers at dinner before the show.

Because she chose to make the **Music Hall** a dinner theatre, Garvin ran into obstacles she hadn't anticipated. "I was very naive," she admits. "I didn't know that liquor licenses couldn't be trans - ferred from one party to another. They don't go automatically with a property when it's sold. I found out. I also found out that due to a Polk Street moratorium on new businesses, all of my food had to be catered. We ran at a considerable deficit for the first six weeks while I dealt with that setback."

The little man in the Sunday *Examiner-Chronicle* pink section jumped out of his seat with enthusiasm over *Dance Between the Lines*, and of course Garvin had no complaints about that. She says that customers who called for reservations consistently mentioned (when asked how they heard about the production) that they were encouraged to attend by the position of the little man. Garvin was troubled, however, by the *Examiner*'s mini-review which appeared every Friday and which was uncomplimentary. She thinks this hurt her business. "I talked to my lawyer about the problem. I see no reason why an unfavorable review has to appear again and again, especially when a performance may have improved since the critic initially reviewed the show. But I couldn't do much about the situation."

Garvin agrees with Kirk Frederick that the cover of *Key* can give a boost to a show. She had opportunity to buy the cover one week during the month of July. "We had a big business pickup," she says.

Steve Baffrey's review on KCBS television was also a help to *Dance Between the Lines*. "Many audience members told us that they'd seen Baffrey on KCBS, heard him praise the show, and were encouraged to attend as a result of his comments.

With a staff of twenty-eight, was it posible for Garvin to pay everybody a living wage? "Everybody got a straight salary," she says. "I've known of too many cases in musical shows, small thea - tres and such, where the dancers were the last to be compensated. I didn't want that to happen at the **Music Hall**, at least while I was running the show."

Dance Between the Lines played at the theatre on Larkin Street, with dancer replacements now and then, for the better part of four years. Garvin took her dancers to Los Angeles, where her show was not so well received nor as popular as it proved to be in San Francisco. In early 1986 the **Music Hall** housed a show called *A Class Act*, a concept which permitted audience members to join a group onstage who were supposedly taking a dance class.

A recent syndicated article stated that, out of more than sixty productions offered during the New York season of 1980-'81, only three plays turned a profit. That's about five percent that could be called successful from a business standpoint. The percentage of shows performed in San Francisco that show a profit over a similar period, I would venture to say, is about the same.

One of the successful shows with which I've been associated in San Francisco over the past thirty years was a production of Terence Rattigan's *Separate Tables* in the spring of 1959. The play had recently closed on Broadway, a road company starring Geral-dine Page had been scheduled to play here but had been cancelled, and the rights to the drama became available for a local production. This was a hot property, a play with artistic merit which was commercially viable. The very week we opened, however, a movie version with an all-star cast also opened at a downtown cinema. We were afraid that the film would kill our business. To our surprise, however, we discovered that the advertising for the film actually helped our production at the box-office. People were interested to compare the play with the movie. Since our production also happened to be very good and received favorable reviews, we came out a winner. We did sell-out business.

You might say, then, that although *Separate Tables* was well performed and the critics liked it, there were other factors that helped the show to financial success. You might say that the timing was just right, or that we were simply lucky.

Not too lucky, however. The Lord giveth and the Lord taketh away. While *Separate Tables* was selling out at the box-office, the production was forced to close. Booked into the **Contemporary Dancers Center** on Washington Street for a limited run, we could not extend our engagement because definite dates had been set to use the theatre for upcoming dance concerts. No place could be located, either, where we could move the show to continue.

Over the years this has been one of the disheartening things about independent production in San Francisco. Even when you have a hit, you can't always get the most out of it, for reasons be-yond your control.

But when people decide to go into the theatre or show busi-ness, nobody promises them a rose garden. A fortunate few some-how do manage, in one way or another, to pick up a bouquet along the path and to disregard the thorns attached to the loveliest of blooms. That's what keeps producers, directors and actors going, in San Francisco as well as throughout the world.

6

BLANKETS, MIKADOS AND MIMES

Some long-running productions and production companies are of such unique nature, without being ethnic or easily classified, that they deserve a space and a chapter of their own.

In the early 70s a group of street performers led and directed by a man named Steve Silver put on crazy costumes and extravagant headdresses and opened a musical revue at the **Savoy Tivoli** called *Beach Blanket Babylon*. The campy humor of this show caught the immediate fancy of San Franciscans, soon developed a cult follow - ing, and within a short time, after a few performances in other loca - tions, moved into a permanent home at the **Club Fugazi**, 678 Green Street. A star was born in the person of Nancy Bleiweiss who, in a ridiculous Carmen Miranda tutti-frutti hat that reached halfway to the ceiling and speaking fractured English in a Spanish accent, delighted audiences that packed the theatre for weekend per - formances. Critics wrote love letters to Bleiweiss, Silver and the whole company and gave the show special awards. Tourists and even celebrities such as Beverly Sills adored *BBB* and saw it again and again. In a brief time the young performers in the show were genuinely famous on the local scene. The fashionable question at cocktail parties was no longer, "Have you seen Beach Blanket Babylon?" but "How many times have you seen it?"

Within recent years other editions, following much the same formula, have been presented at the **Club Fugazi**—*Beach Blanket Babylon Goes Bananas, Beach Blanket Babylon Goes to the Stars, Beach Blanket Babylon Goes Around the World*, and on and on. Nancy Bleiweiss and her sister Roberta, and most of the original *BBB* cast have departed the show, but the same campy spirit of the production continues. Silver claims that even each edition of the revue is in constant flux, with cast changes and new numbers being added and old numbers dropped. So a theatregoer might attend a performance on one particular night and go back six months later to see an entirely different show, even though the first title remains.

Babylon, in any of its versions, however, is now a San Francisco institution and the cast even performed in the **Opera House** for Queen Elizabeth and Prince Philip when they visited the city. Steve Silver, it is said, has become a millionaire. Though the show is non-union, all performers and technicians are paid per - sonnel.

The oldest and, some might say, most successful producing group in San Francisco is the **Lamplighters Opera West Foun - dation** which, by the time this book reaches print, will be close to its thirty-fifth birthday. Founded in 1952 by Orva Hoskinson and Ann Pool, the **Lamplighters** now stage their performances at the **Presentation Theatre**, 2350 Turk Boulevard in San Francisco, as they have done for almost two decades.

Spenser Beman, an executive director of the company, says that "no special philosophy governs the choice of productions, ex - cept that the group is devoted mainly to presenting Gilbert and Sullivan operettas, and works of other operetta composers. Most people think the **Lamplighters** produce only Gilbert and Sullivan works, but actually the company has staged *The Merry Widow, Die Fledermaus* and numerous other light operas. An additional purpose of the organization is to provide opportunities for young singers, designers and various kinds of artisans to develop their skills.

Since 1952 the company has staged hundreds of productions in public parks and on tour as well as at the **Presentation Theatre**. Generally three productions are staged each year, with performances on the weekend. Roles are frequently double cast. No performers are paid.

85

The major part of the company's funding comes from sub-scriptions and contributions. The San Francisco Hotel Tax Fund provides about seven percent of a season's income. Fourteen per-cent comes from special fundraising activities. Everything else comes from individual box-office sales and receipts from tours.

The **Lamplighters** consider *Iolanthe* and *Yeoman of the Guard*, both Gilbert and Sullivan operettas, to be among their most successful productions. The popular group usually plays to full houses in its five hundred seat theatre.

At its yearly awards ceremony in March 1981, the **Bay Area Theatre Critics Circle** presented a special trophy to the **Lamp-lighters** for their outstanding work in the city during the past three decades.

The **Mime Troupe** has the distinction of being San Francis-co's second oldest theatre company. Founded in 1959 by R. G. Davis, under the aegis of the **Actor's Workshop**, the company went independent in 1961. Since the group tours the greater part of the year and appears in public parks and various theatres and audi-toriums, it has no permanent performing space, although a local office and studio have been maintained.

The **Mime Troupe** is a full time, year around company which has grown to a current total of thirty-six actors who are part of a collective under union contract. (After long negotiations, **Actors Equity** and bargaining representatives of the troupe came to an agreement which gives the company full status as an **Equity** com-pany.) A board of directors is elected by the company at large. The **Mime Troupe** has had non-profit corporate status since 1965.

The company usually produces two shows each year. Most of the plays are original, although some works of Brecht and Dario Fo have been presented. The plays are political-social in nature, dealing with issues of current interest such as the economy, racism and the threat of war, "with the aim of uniting the people against the profit-makers and powermongers." Productions usually combine elements of mime, vaudeville, slapstick, epic theatre and musical comedy.

Hundreds of performances of each play are presented on tour throughout California, the Midwest, the east coast and Europe on a regular cycle. Summer performances are given every Saturday and Sunday for a season of several weeks in Golden Gate Park in San Francisco.

William Ball, founder and original director of the American Conservatory Theatre.
(Photo: Larry Merkle)

Marsha Mason and Peter Donat in A.C.T.'s *A Doll's House*, 1972-'73. (above; Photo: Hank Kranzler)

A.C.T.'s 1971-'72 production of *Private Lives* starred Michael Learned and Paul Shenar. (facing page, above; Photo: Hank Kranzler)
Fredi Olster and Marc Singer in William Ball's A.C.T. production of *The Taming of the Shrew*, 1973-'74. (facing page, below; Photo: Hank Kranzler)

Playwright Edward Albee took strong exception to William Ball's "distorted" version of his *Tiny Alice*. There were threats of suits and counter suits all during the season of 1975-'76, but the production continued to play to packed houses, played out its run, and the case never came to court. (Seen in the photo at the right are players Hope Alexander-Willis, Nicholas Courtland, Earl Boen, Anthony S. Teague and Sydney Walker.)

(Photo: A.C.T. Collection)

A 1981 portrait of the San Francisco Mime Troupe (above; Photo: Hazel Hankin). Eric Morris and Laurel Rice were leading players in the Lamplighters' production of *H.M.S. Pinafore*, 1980-'81 season. (below; Photo: Ron Sherl)

Richard Burton in *Camelot* at the Golden Gate Theatre, 1980-'81 season.

Nancy Bleiweiss, star of the original *Beach Blanket Babylon*.
(Photo: Babylon Collection)

Angela Lansbury, star of *Sweeney Todd*, 1981. (Photo: Martha Swope)

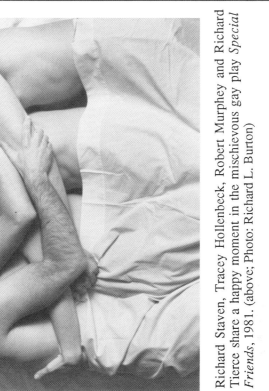

Richard Staven, Tracey Hollenbeck, Robert Murphey and Richard Tierce share a happy moment in the mischievous gay play *Special Friends*, 1981. (above; Photo: Richard L. Burton)

Liza Feldman and Juliet Mills in the thriller *Wait until Dark* at the Alcazar, 1979. (right; Photo: William Ganslen)

Lynn Eldredge, Richard Roemer and Scott Rankine camp it
up Latino style in *Champagne
. . . in a cardboard cup!*, 1980.
(above; Photo: Kirk Frederick)

Peter Coyote and Linda Hoy
headed the cast of *An Autobiography of a Pearl Diver* at
the Magic Theatre, 1978-'79.
(left; Photo: Magic Collection)

Lynn Redgrave in *Sister Mary Ignatius Explains It All for You*,
Marines Memorial Theatre, 1984. (Photo: Ed Krieger)

Errol Ross, Luis Oropeza, Lori Holt, Chuck La Font, Jenny Sterlin,
Drew Eshelman and Sigrid Wurschmidt (left to right) whoop it up in
Cloud Nine, 1983, above. Chuck La Font and Sigrid Wurschmidt in
the Eureka's *Cloud Nine*, 1983, below. (Both Photos: Allen Nomura)

Carlos Kuhn and Thomas-Mark were leading players in Daniel Curzon's *Beer and Rhubarb Pie* at Theatre Rhinoceros, 1980-'81. (above; Photo: Rink)

Alice Thompson and Terry Baum in the Sharpened Spoons production of *Dos Lesbos*, 1981. (below; Photo: Marek A. Majewski)

Marga Gomez, Michele Linfante, Reno and Vicki Lewis in the Lilith production of *Pizza*, 1980. (Photo: Jan Dimarinus)

The **Mime Troupe** has no regular funding source, but it has received support at various times from several foundations. It does receive a grant from the local Hotel Tax Fund. But the major portion of the company's income is from box-office receipts, passing the hat at outdoor performances, and from private donations.

The **Bay Area Theatre Critics Circle** presented the **Mime Troupe** with a special award in 1980, recognizing the company's unique contribution to San Francisco and world theatre.

7

WOMEN, MINORITIES
AND OCCASIONALS

Some theatre companies in San Francisco have been founded in order to provide creative opportunities for artists who are mem - bers of certain ethnic or minority groups, or who are otherwise dis - abled or prevented from participating in the programs of other orga - nizations. Often the plays produced by these companies deal with subjects that appeal or speak directly to the minority group to which the members belong, although this is not always the case.

These kinds of companies also produce sporadically, and seldom operate with regular schedules. Some of them exist and stay in business for several years; others have a flurry of activity for a season or two and then fade from the scene. In these pages I have attempted to list and give information about groups which are representative of these areas. I do not claim to have chronicled all such companies; even some that I mention could not be contacted for updated information or have not responded to my requests for photographs and further data.

According to **Theatre Communications Center of the Bay Area**, the only women's group currently producing in San Francisco is a company called **Lilith**. Based on the belief that there are four times as many parts for men as for women in the traditional theatre repertoire and that many of the roles that do exist for women depict them only as passive spectators rather than active participants in the world, **Lilith** is committed to "exploring through theatre the dilemmas facing a society in transition" because "people need to see women's activities as important and dramatic." The company's office is in the **Women's Building**, 3543 18th Street in San Francisco. Each year the group performs two or three months in the Bay area and then spends several months touring. **Lilith** has played not only up and down the west coast in universities, prisons and small community centers, but was also on European tour in 1979. The company has non-profit corporate status and is funded by several different organizations, businesses, and donations from individuals.

Les Nickelettes is a women's group which was founded in 1972 and which presents plays, skits and cabaret performances that celebrate feminine values through verbal and visual imagery, music and humor. (Last listed phone number for this group is now disconnected.) **It's Just a Stage** is a women's company, founded in 1974, which provides opportunity for women to gain experience and training in theatre arts. All plays are written and performed by women. The emphasis in this group is on a balance between movement and speech in the theatre. Performances are usually staged only in the spring months, in rented spaces. Mailing address of the company is 214 Valencia Street, San Francisco, CA 94103. Telephone: (415) 863-3254. **Sharpened Spoons**, one of the newest of the women's groups, was founded in November, 1980 by Terry Baum, Carolyn Myers and Alice Thompson. I found the company's telephone number disconnected in 1986, but the group's last mailing address was 545 Douglass Street, San Francisco, CA 94114.

Until recently San Francisco did not have a steadily producing black theatre company, although Danny Duncan's independent production of *The Amen Corner* at the **Buriel Clay Theatre** in the **Western Addition Cultural Center** was a great success in the late 70s, and Duncan's *Pinocchio Jones* and *Generations* were also well received at the **Bay View Opera House Theatre**, built in 1885 and renovated in 1975 when it reopened as a cultural center. *Generations* later moved to the **Alcazar** where it had a short run in the larger theatre. Leola Jiles, now receiving renown as a cabaret artist, was a featured player in Duncan's productions.

It has remained for Stanley E. Williams' **Lorraine Hansberry Theatre** to take over the mantle of the only black theatre company producing on a regular basis in San Francisco in the 1980s. Founded in 1981 this company has built an enviable rep - utation for itself in a short period of time, not only with its seasonal schedule of major productions but also with its workshops, staged readings of new works by black writers, and its tours to outlying communities. The company has received numerous critical awards. A new play, *LBJ*, was a particular success in the 1985-'86 season. By continuing to advance as a leading center for the presentation of contemporary black drama, often with inter-racial casting, the **Lorraine Hansberry Theatre** contributes to the economic vitality of the Bay area by providing employment opportunities to black actors, technicians, designers, writers and directors, and further en - hances San Francisco's reputation as a first-rate center of the arts. The company has occupied a space at the **Trinity Episcopal Church**, Bush and Gough Streets, but *LBJ* was presented at the **San Francisco Repertory** space, 19th and Collingwood.

From time to time, a company has emerged on the local level that has chosen to devote itself to the works of William Shake - speare. Such a group was the **New Shakespeare Company**, headed by Margrit Roma, which toured and which, in its later years, changed its name to **Shakespeare San Francisco** and performed for a season or so in Golden Gate Park under Roma's direction. Roma was separated from the company in 1985 and company mana - ger Bobby Winston hired Michelle Truffaut to direct the 1985 sea - son. In 1986 Winston hired Angela Gordon and Ken Grantham to direct the two plays which were presented in the park on weekends, free of charge to the public.

In a previous chapter I have discussed independent gay pro - ductions, and perhaps here I should say something about the kinds of shows staged by the **Society for Individual Rights** in the 1960s and early 70s. All-male musicals such as *Once upon a Mattress*, for example, in which both male and female roles were played by men, resulted in a series of independent productions such as *Mame* and *Applause!* which were staged at **California Hall** on Polk Street as well as other locations. Some might argue that these shows were not strictly gay productions, since they did not deal with gay themes, but they were definitely all male with a good por - tion of the performers in drag. Charles Pierce, who bills himself in cabarets as a "male actress," played the Lauren Bacall role in *Applause!* to the delight of his fans, many of whom are hetero -

sexual as well as homosexual. Another popular female impersonator, known on stage simply as Michelle, scored a great success with his portrayal of the leading role in *Hello, Dolly!*

The **Earnest Players**, a gay theatre company, was founded in November, 1978, and produced shows for a few seasons. This group did not have a home base but usually presented its shows at the **Gumption Theatre**, 1563 Page Street. Despite the pressure to join what could be called the gay mainstream this group headed more and more toward risky productions, plays by unknown playwrights on themes which might be controversial even within the gay community. Ron Tierney was the artistic director of the **Earnest Players**, a group which is now inactive.

The **Gay Theatre Collective** was, in one sense, an improv group since its shows were developed by the members and were based on events in their own lives. But the results were presented as finished theatre pieces. Founded in 1976, the **Collective** had great success with its first production, *Crimes against Nature*, which won several awards from the **Bay Area Critics Circle**. It also had favorable response to its 1980-'81 production of *Contents under Pressure*. The group maintained a permanent staff but had no individual artistic director. Despite its critical and popular acclaim, the **Collective** disbanded and no longer produces on the local theatre scene.

Theatre Rhinoceros is probably the best known and most successful of all the gay theatre companies, and it performs on a much more regular schedule than most, with subscriptions sold on a season's program announced in advance. The group was founded in 1977 by Alan Estes and his administrative director Larry Baugniet. Its productions are now presented in the **Redstone Building**, 2926 16th Street at South Van Ness Avenue in San Francisco. A board of directors is elected by the membership. **Theatre Rhinoceros** is a non-profit corporation whose primary purpose is "to produce plays that provide both a positive image of gay life and a cultural identity for gay people." Alan Estes, now deceased, has been replaced by Kris Gannon as artistic director, and with a woman at the head of this company there are indications that future productions will be more female oriented than they have been in the past. The company does encourage new playwrights and presents play readings and productions of one acts. Performances are on the weekends only.

The **Asian-American Theatre Company** is one of two known similar groups in the United States. It was founded in 1973, has a regular season with performances Thursdays through Sundays, and does a half dozen shows each year. Its major objective is to train Asian-Americans in the various theatre arts of acting, directing, staging and playwriting. The group has a permanent paid staff. For a time the office and performing space was a store front on outer California Street, but the company now performs at the **People's Theatre Coalition** at **Fort Mason**.

The **Irish Theatre Company** of San Francisco was started in 1976 by, suitably enough, a group of Irish actors. The company has performed in various spaces throughout the city but hopes to settle in a permanent space eventually. The group's philosophy is to present Irish plays by authors such as Sean O'Casey, John M. Synge, W. B. Yeats, Samuel Beckett and Hugh Leonard. Door sales have so far been the only means of funding. A telephone conversation with Frank Ahern, former president of the group, reveals that the company is presently inactive with no immediate plans to announce.

Theatre Unlimited has provided performing opportunities for disabled actors. Founded in 1977, the group has non-profit status with special funding. A large staff of permanent, paid administrators and performers is maintained, with Warren R. McCommons and David Lovis serving as the group's directors. There is a regular performing season of mainly original plays. In early 1986 the company toured Bay area schools with its production of *Alice in Wonderland*. Some performances are presented at the **Recreation Center for the Handicapped**, 207 Skyline Boulevard, San Francisco, 94132. Another company which has performed for handicapped people, with all shows signed for the deaf, is **Pacific Arts Theatre**, founded in 1979. Last listed mailing address for this group was 16 Orben Place, San Francisco, 94115.

The **Tale Spinners** is a producing company founded with an intent to produce plays that attempt to bridge the generation gap, present a more positive view of seniors to younger people and in general aid understanding of seniors by destroying myths and breaking down stereotypes. Of late, however, the group has attempted to broaden its goals and has presented plays of other types. In late 1985 its production of *Working* was presented in the **San Francisco Repertory** space at 19th and Collingwood.

Founded in 1975 with Barbara Graham as its original director, the **Tale Spinners** maintains an office c/o **Feedback Productions**, Building D, **Fort Mason**, San Francisco, 94123.

It is proper to mention here, I think, the **People's Theatre Coalition** which, while not a performing group in itself, is an umbrella organization that advises, guides and helps many of the companies listed above and mentioned in other sections of this book. The **People's Theatre Coalition** chooses to sponsor the - atre which is "created by non-traditional theatre makers and/or theatre which is created for non-traditional theatregoing audiences." This means that it looks for work by Third World communities or any community which is disenfranchised from mainstream theatre, such as the disabled community, the women's community and the gay community. It looks for theatre that voices the concerns and experiences of these communities and provides quality enter - tainment. It has also sponsored historical and documentary drama. The **People's Theatre Coalition** makes forty percent of its in - come from space rentals, special programming events and conces - sion sales. The remaining amount comes from local foundations and individual contributors. The board of directors is comprised of the executive directors of the member companies and one representative from its individual members. These people serve on two commit - tees, finance and programming, which are themselves comprised of smaller committees. The **People's Theatre Coalition** is located in Building B, on the third floor, at **Fort Mason**, and has occupied this space since 1979.

Several experimental and improvisational groups, categorized by the **Bay Area Theatre Critics Circle** as those engaging in production styles headed in New Directions, produce sporadically in and around San Francisco. Most of them are without stationary or permanent homes. Their shows, however, often have artistic merit and attract favorable attention. I cannot attempt to deal with all such groups or individual performances which are staged here irregularly, but I will supply a selective list of those which have perhaps most distinguished themselves.

The **Pickle Family Circus**, with offices at 400 Missouri Street in San Francisco, was founded in 1974 and currently maintains a large staff of paid personnel. This company tours fall through spring with a delightful one-ring comedic production of mime, dance and circus.

Duck's Breath Mystery Theatre and the **National Theatre of the Deranged** are probably two of the best-known, best loved and most brilliant improvisational groups now working in San Francisco, as well as other places. In an earlier chapter I have already mentioned the legendary improv group called **The Committee**, which is probably the most famous of all such companies that have entertained San Francisco audiences. **Femprov**, as the name implies, is a women's group founded in 1979 which performs irregularly in cafes throughout the city, as does **The Flash Family Spontaneous Theatre. The Improv Alternative, The Next Stage, Screaming Memes** and **Spaghetti Jam** are all improvisational groups which have done shows, sometimes based on audience suggestions, in theatres and schools and clubs such as the **Old Spaghetti Factory** in North Beach. **Faultline**, a relatively new group, has won critical raves.

In recent years a kind of theatre which, for lack of a better term, is now called "performance art" has become popular with certain audiences. This type of theatre eliminates the actor and any kind of dialogue or plot, as a rule, and concentrates mostly on audio and visual effects. Apart from **Soon 3, Antenna, Motion, The Blake Street Hawkeyes** and one or two other regularly performing companies, there have been individual showings of George Coates' works, most recently his *RareArea* which has been called "fanatically beautiful" and "stunning" by various critics, and Tony Pellegrino's mask drama *Deer Rose*, based on the author's relationship with his dying mother. These kinds of shows are eminently satisfying to a cult audience which has grown larger in San Francisco over the past decade.

The city is also not without its children's theatre companies. **The Next Stage** performs in theatres and schools, and the **San Francisco Children's Opera** gives occasional performances at the **Herbst Theatre** on Van Ness Avenue. Ross and Lou Ann Graham were leaders in children's theatre here for some time with their **Attic Theatre** company, but they went bankrupt in the early 80s. A number of fundraisers and administrators who had worked with the Grahams formed a new group called **The Young Performers Theatre** which has just completed its fourth season.

8

WHICH CRITIC CAN YOU TRUST?

Frank Rich and John Simon are the syphilis and gonorrhea of theatre. . . .
Destructive criticism—well, one wonders what kind of person wants to
spend his life engaged in that kind of profession.

— David Mamet, playwright

Read as little as possible of aesthetic criticism. Such things are either
partisan views, petrified and grown senseless in their lifeless duration, or
they are clever quibblings in which today one's view wins and tomorrow
the opposite.

— Rainer Maria Rilke, *Letters to a Young Poet*

Critics should start being the audience during a rehearsal period and learn
what happens there. Sometimes their lack of knowledge is so incredible. If
they were to be reviewed back by actors, you know, we could put them to
shame.

— Liv Ullmann, Hollywood *Drama-Logue*

There is one thing that 99% of all critics share with one another: they are
failures. I don't mean failures as critics—my God, that's understood. I
don't even mean they are failures as people; I mean something more
painful by far. These people are failures in life.

95

You're a regular theatregoer, either a resident or a visitor in San Francisco, and you'd like to take in a show at one of the local theatres. It's easy enough to find out what's playing, all right, but which reports of these shows can best guide you in deciding which play you want to see? Whose opinions can you trust? Just how far can a theatregoer trust *any* critic's judgment, anyway?

The majority of actors, playwrights, directors and other theatre workers regard critics in general with wariness, dis-ease and, in some cases, with open hostility. The reasons for this are obvious. Critics, through their publications or broadcasts, have open pipe - lines of communication with the public. Whether or not they have the power to make or break a production, or make or break an indi - vidual career, may be questionable, but they do influence public opinion quite strongly. This is because a lot of readers, even sophis - ticated people who should know better, have been conditioned to believe that whatever appears in the newspapers or whatever is announced on radio or television must be the truth, simply be - cause—well, because it appears in the newspapers and is announced on radio and television. Since working theatre artists do not have the same media available, the same pipelines of communication with the public as the critics have, they have no way to defend themselves when they feel they have been unjustly criticized. In fact, they would be considered undignified even if they attempted to defend themselves, through whatever means. Is it any wonder that actors, playwrights and directors regard critics as their natural enemies?

Few performers escape being raked over the coals by the press, at one time or another in their careers. In the first chapter of this book are quotes from critics who chided even such legendary figures as Edwin Booth and Maurice Barrymore over flaws in their work, or because of presumed lapses or inadequacies. Can you ima - gine how hurt and bewildered or enraged Booth or Barrymore must have felt when he read these comments about himself? And how frustrated and impotent he must have felt, too, because he had no way to respond to the critics and no way to defend himself against their diatribes? Well, things haven't changed so much in the last cen - tury. Theatre artists still have to put up with unfavorable and fre - quently unjust reviews, and sometimes they are subjected to vicious, close-to-libelous attacks. Still, there's nothing they can do about it.

Eva Le Gallienne, an actress admired and respected by many, tells in her autobiographies how the eminent New York critic George Jean Nathan never once gave her a favorable review when her career was in its heyday during the 1920s, 30s and 40s. (While others praised her, Nathan continued stubbornly to refer to Le Gallienne, rather deprecatingly, as "the theatre's most talented ama - teur.") Laurence Olivier once comforted Charlton Heston, who had received an extremely unflattering review over a stage performance, by saying, "Never mind the critics, old boy. They don't know fuck- all!" The attitudes of many San Francisco theatre workers towards critics today in the 1980s are contained in comments in a later chap - ter in this book. I think you'll find these observations significant and informative.

Nevertheless, as actress Fionulla Flanagan put it, speaking to an audience when she was in San Francisco in March, 1979 to ac - cept an award from the **Bay Area Theatre Critics Circle**, "I don't like it myself—but we do have to accept the fact that critics *are* a part of the theatre."

The big question to those of us who are theatregoers is: how seriously should we take critics' opinions in deciding on which plays and productions we will attend? Shall we conclude that, be - cause Bernard Weiner of the *Chronicle* says that *Images and Idols* presented by the **Podunk Far-Out Theatre Company** at the **Intersection** is a marvellous, vital piece of theatre, that this play should go at the top of our must-see list? Should we stay away from the touring company of *Sweeney Todd* at the **Golden Gate Theatre** because Gerald Nachman didn't like it? Or should we find some other way of making our decisions, of deciding which plays we'll attend and which we won't?

It might be appropriate here, since it seems inevitable that critics' opinions will affect all of us to a certain degree, to consider what constitutes "good" criticism and "bad" criticism and, indeed, what qualifications a person should have, ideally, to become a critic or a feature writer about the theatre on a major publication. Just who are these people who function as critics and drama reporters on newspapers, magazines, television and radio in the San Francisco Bay area? What backgrounds do they have which entitle them to tell the public what is fine theatre and what isn't? How do certain men and women get to be critics in the first place?

In September, 1980, I was invited to speak on the art of dra - matic criticism at a special conference sponsored by the **California Arts Council** in Sacramento. (I was invited to speak, I'm sure, because at that time I was not only a columnist and critic-reporter for Hollywood *Drama-Logue* but was in my second term as president of the **Bay Area Theatre Critics Circle**.) I stated five qualifica - tions which, in my estimation, a competent critic and drama reporter should have. As I read my speech again today I find that I haven't changed my mind much. I still think these qualifications are valid and important. Bear in mind, of course, that the views I express here are personal opinions, but I suggest that they might be educated opinions since I have spent more than a half century in the theatre in several capacities, including that of critic and reporter. With the exception of a few newcomers on the scene, most of the San Fran - cisco critics are men and women whom I know on a social as well as a professional level. Over a period of many years I have therefore had opportunity to observe these men and women in informal situa - tions, to hear their off-the-cuff comments in which they have ex - pressed their basic attitudes, and I think possibly this has given me special insight concerning their merits and deficiencies.

First, the person who wishes to become a fine theatre critic should not only have a passionate love of the theatre but must also have an appreciation and understanding of many different kinds of theatre. This means, proceeding logically, that the person must know a great deal about the history of the theatre—locally, nationally, and internationally. A good critic always realizes that the theatre is more than one kind of art or entertainment. The theatre is many things. It is the circus and it is Shakespeare in the park; it is Aristophanes' *The Birds* and it is also the latest play by Neil Simon. A just and skillful drama critic evaluates each play within its own period, style and genre, regardless of his or her own personal taste and regardless of what is popular or unpopular at a given moment. The broader a critic's background and knowledge of different kinds of theatre, the more trustworthy and reliable that reviewer's evalu - ation of a particular production will be.

Some people contend that a person doesn't need to have any experience or success in an art field himself to be an able critic of it. But among the best critics of this century one must certainly list such distinguished men as George Bernard Shaw, Stark Young, Harold Clurman and Walter Kerr. Perhaps people who have only an aca -

demic knowledge of acting, directing or playwriting can occasion - ally hit the nail on the head in their reviews, but people who have had failures and learned from them and gone on to successes in an art field best understand its creative process at gut level. They are also less likely to be vindictive in their critiques, because they have less bitterness and envy in them. Shaw, Young, Clurman and Kerr all had successes in the theatre. On a local level Robert Hurwitt who writes for the *East Bay Express* and other publications, A. J. Esta who writes for Hollywood *Drama-Logue*, and Steve Baffrey who reviews shows on KCBS know what they are talking about through personal experience, as does Barbara Bladen of the San Mateo *Times* and Tom Winston of KABL. These people have strong opin - ions, yes, and they can be acerbic at moments, but one finds little personal rancor between the lines of their reviews. Unfortunately one does find rancor between the lines of reviews written by other local critics, some of whom fall into the category of those described by William Goldman in *The Season* as existing on the periphery of show business as critics because they couldn't make a success of it as performers, playwrights or directors. (I hasten to assure readers that all local critics don't fall into this category, but there are two or three who do and they wield a certain amount of power in San Francisco theatre, simply because they have an outlet in the press.)

Second, a conscientious critic will blend objectivity, fair play and a dedication to accuracy in his or her reviews. We might as well admit that there is no such thing as a completely objective critic. Being human, critics bring prejudices, preferences and personal limitations with them when they enter a theatre, even as you and I. "What is obscene to one man is the laughter of genius to another," as D. H. Lawrence put it. However, a critic with integrity has some self-insight; he or she is aware of personal biases and attempts to control or overcome them when evaluating a play or a production or when writing a feature article for publication.

Sins of omission exist in reviewing and drama reporting, as they exist in other aspects of human behavior. Often a critic's pre - judices become obvious, when one stops to think about it, through what he or she *neglects* to say in a review or a feature story. These omissions are seldom apparent to the lay reader, but when one knows the individual critic and his or her prejudices and predilec - tions, the omissions grow increasingly apparent.

A few years ago Steven Winn, one of the *Chronicle*'s review-ers and reporters, did a story on the **Actor's Workshop**, the com-pany which was so prominent on the local scene in the 50s and early 60s. He interviewed actors who had been associated with this company. Within a few days a letter from a reader appeared criticiz-ing Winn for not mentioning Maurice Argent, who had been one of the **Workshop**'s leading actors, in his article. This omission was indeed significant, but no more significant than Winn's failure to mention several other prominent **Workshop** players still living and acting here. Winn's choice of interviewees, with one or two excep-tions, seemed strange. It might be argued, of course, that since he is relatively new in these parts Winn just didn't know to whom he should talk about this company which was so well known in the 50s and early 60s. But doesn't this prove the point I made earlier that the best critics and reporters on theatre activity are those who have a sound knowledge of its history? This knowledge is something which can be gained only with time and solid experience. Unfortu-nately, editors and publishers do not take this fact much into account when they hire their theatre writers, and it is the readers who suffer for it, albeit unknowingly.

In the autumn of 1984 Bobby Lewis, a co-founder with Elia Kazan and Cheryl Crawford of the **Actor's Studio** in New York and one of the most renowned acting teachers in the country, who counts among his students such luminaries as Meryl Streep and Anne Bancroft (who still studies with him) came to San Francisco to give a one-night lecture on modern acting at **Theatre-On-The-Square**. This was not a money making venture for Lewis; he didn't need the money. In fact, he came here at his own expense, at no financial guarantee. Admission price was set at a very low figure, within the reach of everyone. Press releases were sent to the major papers. Weiner of the *Chronicle* and Nancy Scott of the *Exam-iner* were invited to interview Lewis and attend his lecture, if they wished. Neither of them showed the slightest interest. No press release about Lewis's appearance was printed in either the *Chron-icle* or the *Examiner*, although releases about many events of less significance were. A great man came and went, and as far as the major press was concerned he didn't exist. Lewis and his presenters offered an exceptional service to both theatre workers and the San Francisco public at large; Weiner and Scott did local theatre and the public a disservice by ignoring it.

I am well aware that drama editors of leading newspapers are inundated with press releases and requests to attend and review productions all over the Bay area. The *Chronicle* and *Examiner* critics and feature writers have time limitations and also space limitations. They can't print every press release or review every production. But what about standards, when making selections of what to print and what to review? Surely a San Francisco appearance by such an eminent man as Bobby Lewis merited respectful attention by the daily press. But it didn't get it.

Other kinds of omissions occur in reviews themselves, and to one who can read between the lines they reveal the critic's prejudices and lack of knowledge or standards. If, as an example, a critic writes an extensive review of a production of *Hamlet*, praises the sets and costumes and the direction and many of the players, and then in the final paragraph says, "The Prince of Denmark was played by Harry Jones," what does this indicate? I'll tell you what it says to me. It says that the reviewer knows he can't really criticize Harry Jones, because Harry Jones has actually done good work. But (for some personal reason) the critic doesn't want to give Harry Jones credit, either. So he merely lists Harry Jones as "also in the cast." Weiner does this quite often to punish those in his disfavor, and the performer is probably quite hurt by it. It is the reading public, however, which is misled.

David Armstrong, feature writer and sometime theatre critic on the *Examiner*, is a new man on the block and I don't know him personally. But I was interested to read his reports on William Ball's resignation from **A.C.T.** Armstrong's first story on this event was objective and straightforward, a good job of reporting. He simply related the facts. His second and third stories, however, grew more and more slanted. I couldn't help but wonder how and by whom he had been influenced to "interpret" Ball's resignation and to write negatively about **A.C.T.** in general. One of his most blatant sins of omission occurred in a paragraph about Ed Hastings' assignment as Ball's successor. He stated that Hastings' last two directorial jobs for **A.C.T.** had not met with critical approval. True enough. But what about Hastings' long-term service to **A.C.T.** and its audiences, and what about the many shows he directed here over a twenty year period which *were* well received by press and public? Armstrong's omission of positive comments about Hastings' engagement as **A.C.T.**'s new general director was unfortunate. I

101

hope it does not foreshadow the way he will slant stories about **A.C.T.** in the future. (Barbara Shulgasser's subsequent interview with Hastings about his "take-over" at **A.C.T.** was a much more reasonable and balanced *Examiner* feature.)

Press coverage of the February, 1986 "shake-up" at **A.C.T.** revealed more about the writers themselves than the stories did about the event. The *Chronicle* reviewers, in particular, were chortling with glee at the news of Ball's resignation. For days following the director's announcement the only story with a positive slant to appear in the *Chronicle* was an editorial which credited Ball with his accomplishments. Weiner and Winn couldn't wait to stick the knife in Ball's back one more time, two or three more times if possible. Within twenty-four hours of Ball's announcement, to the amuse - ment of actors currently in rehearsal with the director (and who themselves wouldn't presume to analyze Ball's decision or the pos - sible results of it) Weiner had a story in the *Chronicle* telling the general public what it all meant. For days Weiner and Winn, and to a lesser extent Gerald Nachman with his Sunday piece, "A.C.T.'s Rise and Fall," continued to muckrake, printing half-truths and making innuendoes and casting doubts and suspicions and, in general, doing their best to prejudice the public's mind against Ball and **A.C.T.** I don't hesitate to call these stories unconscionable.

A.C.T.'s rise and fall? Who says that this company has fallen? It may be that **A.C.T.** has fewer subscribers than it once had, but its box-office business for Shaw's *You Never Can Tell* and Coward's *Private Lives* in the spring of 1986 couldn't have been much better, with many sold out performances.

Striking a degree of balance, Weiner's Saturday column of March 8, 1986 did mention that the **Eureka Theatre** and the **Magic Theatre** were suffering a slump in business. He reported that on occasion there were only a dozen people in the **Eureka**'s audience for *Gardenia* and that some performances had to be can - celled. But nowhere in the column did Weiner speculate as to the reasons for this box-office slump. He did not report, for example, that the two theatres' choices of plays might not always be the best nor that Susan Marsden's direction of *Gardenia* might be called pedestrian; he did not suggest any administrative or backstage problems with either company; he did not lament the fact that only the administrative staff, directors and technical people earn anything approaching a living wage at the **Magic** and the **Eureka**; he did not mention that many actors and directors have private reasons for not wishing to work with these groups any longer. Weiner likes the **Magic** and the **Eureka**. He would not want to write anything negative about them or criticize them in any way. Their decline in business he simply terms a "mystery."

But is he willing to be specific about problems with **A.C.T.**? You bet he is. For months before William Ball's resignation and for days following it, in the best journalistic style of the *National En-quirer*, Weiner and Winn labeled Ball volatile, temperamental, diffi-cult to work with, unresponsive to the community and a dozen other things. They cast dark clouds over the financial affairs of the com-pany (even though auditors had publicly reported that these affairs were perfectly in order) and derided the salary which Ball was paid. They commented on the number of actors who were no longer with the company. In short, they did everything they could to blacken **A.C.T.**'s reputation in the public mind. The truth is, the public was greatly misled by Weiner and Winn's irresponsible and biased reporting.

I don't claim to know Bill Ball intimately. I don't doubt that, the same as many people, he can be irritable and lose his temper at times. I don't doubt that he was strong-minded and individualistic in his management of **A.C.T.** Most genuine artists are indeed positive personalities. That may be what makes them artists. I don't doubt, either, that Ball was "unresponsive" to certain gentlemen of the press. (There can be good reason for not talking to reporters who misquote you, quote you out of context, or invalidate the opinions you have expressed through innuendoes of their own or quotes from others who are less informed.) But in both my personal and pro-fessional relationship with Ball he never treated me with anything but respect and courtesy, and I never saw him give anyone else less than the same treatment. The rehearsal period for *The Passion Cycle*, in which I played Pontius Pilate, was a joyful experience. As a director he is highly disciplined, yes, and he expects his actors to do their homework, but he is also gentle, compassionate and kind with his performing artists as they go through the rehearsal and discovery process. No negative vibes permeated the air at the studio on Geary Street where we rehearsed *The Passion Cycle*. Ball may have been hurting inside from the way the press was raking him over the coals when he tendered his resignation, but if so no one would have known it. He behaved with the utmost dignity and decorum, and his spirits were good. The entire company applauded him again and again for his creativity as we followed his direction in the staging of the Easter story.

Both Weiner and Winn made much of the fact that Ball earned a good salary, a better salary than artistic directors of other com - panies in the country (Winn went to great length to investigate the salaries of administrators in other cities and to publish figures, as if that proved anything) and noted that while other operating expenses were cut, Ball's salary stayed the same or rose. Well, so what? Big deal. Does Woody Allen, as talented as he may be, make the same money for each film as Robert Redford? Is the artistic director of a San Francisco theatre company due no more money than the admini - strator of a theatre in Denver? As Joan Rivers would say, grow up! Or as my cabaret artist friend Sharon McNight once put it, "There are two words in show business—there's show and there's also business." Most artists, when they mature beyond the provincial thinking of Weiner and Winn, negotiate for the best salaries they can get and they usually get what they're worth. Ball was, and still is, worth a lot to **A.C.T.** (Don't forget, he founded it and built it to its world-wide reputation.) Over the last ten years, have either Weiner or Winn written articles, for example, to inform the public that John Lion of the **Magic** has drawn a living wage as his salary, while actors at this theatre for a long time earned only thirty dollars a week? What about *that* kind of disparity? What about the fact that even today the **Magic** operates on a yearly budget of approximately half a million dollars, but actors are still only paid eighty-five dollars a week? Does Weiner ever write an exposé of that situation? No, he doesn't. In the meantime, even if you concede that Ball's salary might be excessive (and I don't, necessarily) shouldn't it be pointed out that the contract actors at **A.C.T.** do earn a living wage, a sal - ary higher than that paid by any other theatre company in the Bay area, and that they have always earned at least this basic scale since **A.C.T.** came to San Francisco in the middle 60s? But giving credit where credit is due, except in writing about his personal favorites, has never been a notable attribute of Weiner's reportage.

Weiner and Winn have made much, in their various articles, of the actors who have supposedly "defected" from **A.C.T.** Have they forgotten that from the very beginning of the company Ball indicated that a policy of his conservatory was to encourage actors to work elsewhere when they felt the need and to return home to **A.C.T.**

104

when schedules permitted? Over the years, many actors have indeed left the company to work in other theatres and in films and television but that does not mean, necessarily, that they have left in disaffec - tion with Ball or **A.C.T.** itself. There is a natural attrition from season to season with every theatre company. Actors do have a desire to move on, to try their wings in other skies in an attempt to advance their careers. Some artists may be content to spend their lives working in regional theatre; others are more ambitious. Should we label Luis Oropeza, Drew Eshelman or Richard E. T. White as defectors because they no longer work with the **Eureka**? Did Sam Shepard, Peter Coyote, Jim Haynie and playwright Michael McClure defect from the **Magic**? Does the departure of these people from these theatres indicate that there is something sinister and ter - ribly wrong about the management of either the **Magic** or the **Eureka**? I don't think so. Perhaps some of them have had their complaints, as some actors have had their complaints about **A.C.T.** (and as many local actors, God knows, had about the **Actor's Workshop** thirty years ago) but it's all in the natural order of things, this attrition. One door closes, another opens. One era ends, another begins.

All right. Why, one might ask, are Weiner and Winn (and Nancy Scott of the *Examiner*, plus the newcomers who are writing for this paper) so "down" on **A.C.T.**? Why are they so determined to discredit Ball and this company of which San Francisco should be so proud and which is famous throughout the world?

Part of the answer to this question lies in the William Goldman quote at the beginning of this chapter. Part of the answer lies in the fact that Ball probably feels so betrayed by the local press that he won't even talk to them anymore. (Reporters and critics can't stand that; they consider themselves gods before whom everybody should bow.) But another reason lies, I think, in psychological motivations far more complex and subtle. The newer crop of critics and reporters in San Francisco did not "discover" **A.C.T.** The company is not their baby. They don't feel benevolent and supportive, because **A.C.T.** is Establishment. It was a success before they got here. They don't feel they had a part in creating that success, so they have a subconscious need to destroy **A.C.T.** and supplant it with an entirely different company, or at least a different kind of manage - ment. Then they could relate. Then it would be "their" theatre.

Weiner and Misha Berson, who writes for the San Francisco *Bay Guardian*, are cut much from the same cloth. Products of the 60s rebel-culture, they are most comfortable and identify best with socio-political drama. (In fact, Berson, perhaps under editorial order, doesn't often bother to review plays unless they have some social or ethnic significance.) Their preference doesn't bother me greatly; believe it or not, I have a social conscience, too, and I have been associated with many productions which were considered avant-garde and experimental and daring for their time. (I produced and acted in the first west coast production of Sartre's *No Exit* in Seattle in 1951, I directed the first San Francisco production of Jean Genet's *The Maids* in 1959, and I acted here for a solid year in Albee's *The Zoo Story* for the **Actor's Workshop** in 1961-'62, just to give a few examples.) No, it's okay with me if Weiner and Berson have a personal preference for the style of the **Mime Troupe** as opposed to the polish and elegance of **A.C.T.** shows. But Weiner, especially, writes for a reading public with broad tastes. He should have an appreciation of other kinds of theatre and other kinds of actors than those that are his personal favorites if he is to review them objectively for a newspaper which has the largest circulation in northern California. Both Weiner and Berson project their anti-Establishment views between the lines of their critiques.

Paradoxically, Weiner and Berson are exultant when a local boy, one of their discoveries, "makes it" in the big time. When John Vickery or Ed Harris or Joe Spano scores a commercial success on Broadway, in films or on television and then comes home to the Bay area to do a show or make a personal appearance, these reviewers burst their buttons with pride. It never seems to occur to them that these actors are now part of commercial show business just as Marsha Mason and Michael Learned and Marc Singer became when they left **A.C.T.** and just as much Establishment as older actors who went through the New York-Hollywood scene and now live here permanently. But Vickery, Harris and Spano are "their" discov - eries and they identify.

Likewise, they identify with the **Eureka**, the **Magic** and the **One Act Theatre**. They did not discover **A.C.T.**; **A.C.T.** was well founded in San Francisco and a roaring success before the cur - rent major critics arrived on the scene. But they were involved in the growth and development of the smaller theatres; they feel comfortable with them and with their managements. They have no compunction about reporting "irregularities" at **A.C.T.** or attacking William Ball with the most scurrilous kind of name-calling. But did any story appear in the *Chronicle* when Richard E. T. White re - signed as artistic director of the **Eureka** and the acting company split into factions when it came to selecting White's successor? No, that backstage intrigue was kept very hush-hush and no word of the company's inner conflicts was published in the *Chronicle*. Simi - larly, Weiner ran no story about the pressures put on Peter Tripp and the real reasons for his departure from the **One Act**. Nor has there ever been an article under Weiner or Steven Winn's by-line exposing the half million dollar annual budget at the **Magic** with Lion and his staff drawing substantial salaries while actors still work for eighty-five dollars a week. They'll sling the mud at Ball, but they throw nothing but roses at their personal friends.

Well, I have nothing against the **Eureka**, the **Magic** or the **One Act**. I like a lot of the people who work there, too, and I wish them success. But I do not think these theatres are entitled to pref - erential treatment. Some readers might think it's acceptable for Weiner to attack **A.C.T.** because it's a big-time operation and it can take it, and they might think it's noble of Weiner to take it easy on the little guys and nurture them. Twenty years ago I would have bought that philosophy, too, but times have changed and so have working conditions. The **Eureka**, the **Magic** and the **One Act** are now big buck operations. They are still only semi-professional, in the strictest sense of the word, but they enjoy all of the benefits from the press that **A.C.T.** and Shorenstein's shows get; every pro - duction is reviewed, some small theatre productions get even more feature space than full **Equity** shows receive in the daily *Chron - icle* and the Sunday *Examiner-Chronicle*, and no differentiation is made in the theatre guide listings between the rankest amateur show and a full-scale professional production. If small theatres are entitled to all of these benefits, and I don't say they aren't, shouldn't they be subjected to the same kind of scrutiny and investigative reporting that **A.C.T.** has endured? While I don't enjoy muckraking, I think I might find the major press's treatment of Ball and **A.C.T.** a little more tolerable if reporters like Weiner and Winn were equally criti - cal of other theatres in San Francisco.

So much for objectivity, fair play and accuracy among our cur - rent major critics. So much for their sense of balance in reviewing and reporting. I could cite a dozen more examples, sins of omission as well as commission, cases in which they have slanted stories with half-truths and innuendoes, but I choose to move on now to a discussion of other qualities which a competent critic should possess.

A third requisite of an accomplished critic, following a knowledge of theatre history and a sense of accuracy and fair play, is certainly a high degree of perception and insight into the arts of directing and acting.

Few critics, and few audiences for that matter, can differentiate between an actor's contribution to a performance and his director's contribution. Maybe this is as it should be; some authorities contend that the best directing shouldn't be apparent at all, everything that happens on the stage should just unfold naturally and at least believably if not with a high degree of theatrical effectiveness. If it does, then the director has done his work well, claim these theorists. But many actors can cite cases in which they've received little help from their director at all, or have been misguided by their director, and yet they've managed to pull the show together and the critics have given the director more than his share of the credit. Believe me, it happens. Directors can also talk about how actors resist them, or perhaps how they can't get the actor to do what they want him to do and the director gets blamed for it. I do believe that a very fine director can sometimes help a good actor to give a better-than-usual performance, but even a great director can't make a poor actor deliver brilliantly. A silk purse from a sow's ear cannot be made. I guess there's no way to determine with absolute accuracy who gets more credit for a good performance, the director or the actor, or who is more to blame for the poor one, because if we as the audience haven't been present during the rehearsals we don't know what's happened there. My own tendency is to give the greater credit to the actor if his performance is good and credit the director for the general concept of the production, the staging and the overall dynamics of the ensemble work. If the actor gives a weak performance I don't always blame him or her for it entirely; after all, it is the producer or director who has cast the actor in the first place and that's *his* mistake.

A discerning critic, however, should know how to separate the actor's work from the playwright's requirements in evaluating a performance. This is easier to do than to separate the work of the director from that of the actor, but it's surprising how few critics do it successfully. As Sir Richard Attenborough said in an interview in

108

the *Hollywood Reporter*, on December 20, 1985, "What is cruel is that many of the critics—and it displays, in my opinion, their abys - mal ignorance, and they should know more about the job before they behave as arrogantly as some of them have done—do not dif - ferentiate between part and performance. If a script demands that a particular character mope around the theatre in a state of misery and depression and doesn't know what to do and finally says, 'I'm going back,' and the child who plays the part convinces you that she's moping around the theatre, she is doing what is required of her."

Steven Winn reviewed a play called *Blood Relations* in the *Chronicle* in the fall of 1983. This **Tour de Force** production was directed by Andrea Gordon under an **Equity** waiver. The play is about the Lizzie Borden case, and two well-known local **Equity** actors played Lizzie's parents. In his review Winn stated that these two actors gave "tired performances." As it happened, the two ac - tors were playing people who were seventy years of age and, in fact, at one point in the play's dialogue Lizzie says, "You look so tired, Papa!" How would Winn have recommended the two actors portray these roles, bursting with energy? Here's an example of a critic who did a poor job of evaluating the requirements of the roles, not a case of actors performing inadequately. The requirements were even spelled out in the dialogue, and Winn still didn't get the point.

On another occasion Winn reviewed a play at the **Julian** in which he said an actor "had a firm grip on his role" but that the role "atrophied" as the play progressed. This may or may not have been the case. But if the role did indeed atrophy it was in the writing of the part, not in the actor's performance. Winn's single sentence somehow implied that the actor was to blame for the role going downhill, which I don't think he meant. What he could, and should, have done was to give the actor full credit in a single sentence for what he did with the material provided and then, later in the review and well-separated from comments about the actor's work, state what he thought was wrong with the writing. This would have been much clearer and a much fairer critique of the performance.

A good critic should understand and appreciate different styles of acting. Few do. Most San Francisco critics have grown up and been educated to a bastardized Method technique of acting, a scratch-stutter-stumble and fumble system which passes in films and on television as "natural" and "realistic." (Please note that I say "bastardized" Method, because this approach to the art of acting is not what Stanislavski taught, it is not what Maria Ouspenskaya taught when I studied with her, and it is not what Stella Adler and Bobby Lewis teach today.) Consequently, when confronted with any other style—a bravura, larger-than-life style, for example, which the best classical actors have always possessed—these critics belittle it as "affected" or "mannered." The shortcoming, of course, exists not in the actor who is performing in this style but in the critic to whom it is foreign and who does not understand it. Or, to para-phrase and put it another way, the fault, dear Brutus, lies not always in the stars but often in the critics who are their underlings.

The superb Canadian novelist Robertson Davies, who had ex-tensive theatre experience before he took to writing fiction (much of which has a theatre background) was recently quoted in the *Chron-icle*: "Intellectuals are the syphilis of the arts. In the old days, an actor was a man with a rich voice and a splendid emotional range. Nowadays he has a B.A., a subtext and everything but talent."

Think about this pithy comment for a minute. When was the last time you read a review in which the critic remarked about the quality of an actor's voice, either favorably or unfavorably? I don't think I've ever read a comment like that in a San Francisco news-paper. Yet his voice is the actor's greatest tool, especially in classical roles. Read what critics and biographers have said about the legend-ary actors of another age; almost all of them comment about the resonance or the power and range of the actors' voices. Don't we have any good voices today? Well, of course we have a few. But acting teachers, with some exceptions, don't stress voice and diction today as much as they once did, and many actors never learn to breathe and phrase and place their tones and articulate properly. Most critics, completely uninformed, never express admiration for an eloquent voice in their reviews and, just as bad, they never seem to consider nasalities and poor articulation a detriment to an actor. There is one Bay area actor who whines, I mean really snivels and *whines* his way through every performance, no matter what sort of a character he's playing, yet Bernard Weiner never mentions this and invariably gives the man a rave notice.

A certain test of an actor lies not only in his natural vocal equipment but in the skill with which he uses it. Does he project the same quality in every role he plays, as does the man I mentioned in the last paragraph, or does he vary his vocal tones? Does he use high pitches and low pitches, as required by the character he is playing? Can he produce a raw guttural effect when required, as well as a smooth cultured tone, without injuring his vocal cords? Is he adept at various dialects? Once or twice Weiner has criticized an actor's dialect, or lack of it, and I do recall one time when he complimented an actor on his diction, but I have never read a review by a San Francisco critic in which he commented on an actor's speech pattern as befits the character he is playing or noted that a different speech pattern might be desirable.

Most critics do not understand the finer points of character - ization. The best actors are those who can play a wide variety of parts. These actors change not only their vocal patterns for each role, but they also try to move differently and, when possible, they give each character a somewhat different look. An actor who does this is a genuine artist and not just a personality performer, and he should be so recognized by the critics. But have you ever read a review by a San Francisco critic in which he lauded an actor's ver - satility, or pointed out how or why the actor seems different in one part from another? I haven't. Of course, many actors are victims of type casting (which is not always their fault) and they may have fewer opportunities to develop. But many play themselves over and over again because they don't know how to do otherwise. A real artist, however, characterizes and his talent can only be fairly evaluated when he has been seen in a variety of roles and when the body of his work is considered. If our San Francisco critics are aware of this they seldom give evidence of it.

Clarity in writing style is the fourth requisite, in my opinion, for good criticism. There's no need for a critic or a reviewer to use esoteric language, to try to impress readers with how many ten syllable words exist in his vocabulary. Be a little suspicious, then, of the critic whose writing style is overly literary or academic. He's more interested in arranging words on paper than he is in what he's supposed to be telling his readers.

A critic who uses too many abstract adjectives, who describes the costumes as "beautiful" or so-and-so's performance as "stun - ning," isn't really telling the reader much, unless further comment explains *why* the costumes were beautiful or the actor's perfor - mance was stunning. "Beautiful" and "stunning" may mean very different things to a reader than they do to a critic.

111

Additionally, a critic who too often describes performances, especially those given in small theatres or **Equity** waiver houses, as "brilliant" or "thrilling" should be taken with a grain of salt. If *Examiner* critic Barbara Shulgasser gives three or four stars indis-criminately to productions she sees in somebody's basement in the Mission district, labeling that performance as "superb," what adjec-tives and what rating system does she have left to describe Laurence Olivier's performance when he comes to town in *King Lear*? It's all very well to encourage bright, young talent, but let's be sensible and maintain some kind of balance while we do it. It is a disservice to young talent to imply that it has already, with little background or experience, scaled the heights and reached the pinnacle of artistic excellence; it is a disservice to suggest to readers that they will see unqualified brilliance when they attend the performance; and it is a disservice to more experienced talent which has paid its dues and justly earned its rewards to imply that all those years of training were meaningless. (Weiner and Misha Berson, of course, love to humble the Establishment with this tactic.) Modest praise for work well done is sufficient; an astute critic will wait for the exceptional performance before employing the most extravagant praises in a review. And, let's face it, truly exceptional performances don't occur that often.

A critic who writes with a sense of humor will be fun to read. Many of us have chuckled over the famous one-liners. "*The House Beautiful* is the play lousy," wrote Dorothy Parker on one occasion. And on another, "In *The Lake*, Katharine Hepburn runs the gamut of emotions from A to B." The *New York Times* reviewer of a pro-duction of *Antony and Cleopatra* said simply, "Last night Tallulah took a barge down the Nile and sank." Still another one-liner not quite so well-known was written by Louis Kronenberger. "It's a very dull trifle," he said, "about a loving but quick-tempered lady concert pianist and a famous novelist. They live together off and on—often on but oftener off, in a way that goes on and on and is all too often awful." The greatest put-down of all, perhaps, was "There was only one thing wrong with the play I saw last night—the curtain was up."

Yes, these are rib-tickling comments and amusing to read, and I'm sure the readers did enjoy them. But were they rational, con-structive criticisms of the performances? Beware of critics who are so enthralled with their own cleverness that they are more concerned with coining delightful phrases than in telling you and me what the play is about, what its good points or what its faults might be, or how the production could be improved. To be witty at the expense of a play or a performer can sometimes be cruel as well as down - right destructive. I suggest that a responsible critic may choose to write in a tone which is light-hearted and breezy, and may make a quip here and there, but will shy away from barbs which aim at the jugular. A playgoer has every right to be suspicious of a critic who is excessively vicious, as for example Weiner and Winn have been in their repeated attacks on William Ball and **A.C.T.**

The final qualification which I consider essential for a good critic is a commitment to social and artistic responsibility. The crit - ic's own standards, demonstrated in reviews, should not merely inform but instruct the readers—without being overly didactic, of course. Sometimes, too, the critic has opportunity to perform a gen - uine service in recommending a theatrical event which is a sleeper and might have escaped the attention of other writers and the public in general. I will give Bernard Weiner credit as one San Francisco reviewer who is conscientious in this regard.

The qualifications for an accomplished critic which I have stated in this chapter represent an ideal, and an ideal which is seldom achieved—in San Francisco or anywhere else. The reason lies in the way most critics are hired for their jobs. Neither they, nor you and I, unfortunately, has much control over this.

Critics are hired by editors and station managers, and they are hired for myriad reasons, few of which have anything to do with genuine expertise in the field. Some are hired because they are literate or entertaining writers, capable of that clever phrase (which doesn't mean, necessarily, that they know what they are writing *about*!) or because a vacancy occurs on the staff of a publication and they have been shifted from, say, the sports page to the drama desk because the editor thinks, "Well, Joe sees a lot of movies. Let's put him in that spot!" And what do you know, miracle of miracles, abracadabra, the former sports writer now becomes the man (or woman) who is absolute authority on the art of the drama and ad - vises thousands of readers what is good and what is not good in this field! If Joe's background and experience are valid qualifications for a job as a critic, then any editor's personal friend is qualified and any idiot who watches television four hours a day is an authority on acting and directing and playwriting. The absurdity of this situation is, of course, apparent to anyone who has a brain in his head.

I do not mean to imply that critics—and most particularly critics in the Bay area—are not nice people, or that they are dolts and without integrity. Many of them are very well-intentioned. What I do say is that, with a few exceptions, they offer opinions and criti - cisms which are laymen's opinions and little more informed than the average theatregoer's—and in some cases, perhaps, not as well in - formed.

A sad effect of the hiring system used by the *Chronicle* and the *Examiner*, publications which do not actively seek qualified people to be their critics but merely announce an opening and consider applications (most often, as I have said, appointing writers from other pages of the paper), and the neighborhood and gay publi - cations which employ almost anybody who applies (because they pay no money and can't get really qualified people), is that the newly appointed people, often very nice human beings, slowly be - come drunk with their own power. Yesterday they were nobody; suddenly they are supplied the means to publicly praise or belittle artists who have spent a lifetime perfecting a craft. They come to believe, I mean really *believe*, that because they interview and write about stars they are stars themselves. Much has been written, many stories have been told about the temperament of actors and directors, but let me tell you, I have observed more prima donna-like and outrageous behavior from critics than I have ever observed from actors. I have seen nice people become monsters, due to the power they wield as representatives of the press and the forum they have available to express their views. It is a deplorable situation from which nobody benefits, least of all the theatre and the playgoing public. The remedy, of course, would be better hiring policies by editors and publishers, but based on experiences I have had in San Francisco over the past thirty years I don't hold much hope for that remedy taking effect during the remainder of this century.

Benedict Nightingale is an American-born gentlemen who spent many years in England studying the traditions of the theatre on that side of the Atlantic and working as a critic of the British stage. He recently spent a year substituting for Walter Kerr, writing a fea - ture article each Sunday for the *New York Times*. In his book *Fifth Row Center* (Times Books, 1986) he comments on what he calls the "appalling" record of dramatic criticism. He comments on the hostility accorded Ibsen's first works, which were labelled "wretched, loathsome, and deplorable," goes on to remind us how the first plays of Harold Pinter and Edward Bond were derided, and asks us to consider George Jean Nathan's persistent refusal to re - spond to the works of Tennessee Williams with anything like the enthusiasm he showed for Eugene O'Neill. "Sensible readers will treat critics very skeptically indeed," Nightingale concludes, "and decent critics will urge them to do so."

This observation is an excellent lead-in to the conclusion of this chapter, as well as an answer to the question posed at the chapter's beginning. Which critic can you trust? None of them, my friends.

Go ahead and read the reviews, if you must, for your amaze - ment as well as your amusement. But try to read as many different reviews as possible. Do not let the mini-review in the pink section of the Sunday *Examiner-Chronicle* or the position of the little man be your sole guide to which show(s) you should or should not see. That little man, jumping out of his chair or slumped in it or absent altogether, reveals the opinion of only one reviewer—and it has been noted that his degree of enthusiasm is often inconsistent with the tone of the original full-length review written by the same critic. So check on what a few other critics have to say. Try to talk to somebody who may have seen the show. The reactions of a casual theatregoer are often less biased than those of the professional critic.

If, however, you don't have access to a collection of reviews or you can't find anybody who's already seen the show (or even if you have) it's probably a good idea to consider some other factors before you plunk your money down for a ticket. Does the content of the play—its theme or subject matter—sound as if it might be appealing to you? (It might not appeal to the *Chronicle* critic, but it might be right down your alley. Or the *Examiner* critic might love it, but it's the type of show that turns you off completely.) Let the general theme or story line give you a hint as to whether or not you'd enjoy seeing the play. Have you seen any other plays by the same playwright? Maybe the critics don't like his work, but you do. If so, you should book your seats, no matter *what* the critics have had to say about it. What about the director and the leading actors? If they are familiar to you and you've appreciated them before, there's a good chance you'll enjoy their efforts again. If their work has left you cold on previous occasions—well, you might want to give them another chance, if the play itself sounds interesting. No artists score

115

bulls-eyes all the time, and performers improve with experience and just plain living.

In any case, be an individual and make up your own mind about what you want to see. Yes, it takes a litle effort, but your energies will be well spent. How many times, in your theatregoing experience, have you attended a production which the critics, and perhaps even your friends, have raved about and you've been disappointed in it? How many times, too, have you seen a show that a lot of people disliked and you've rather enjoyed it? This has happened to all of us. Contrary to popular myth, the majority is not always right. Have the courage to follow your own instincts.

Nobody has ever put it better than Shakespeare. "To thine own self be true" is still sound advice, even in making a decision about how to spend an evening. You don't have to rush to see, and subsequently love, every show about which the critics have waxed enthusiastic. Nor must you turn thumbs down on everything which the critics have hated. You might find value or entertainment in a show which others have missed. Trust yourself and gamble a little. Take a chance. The rewards to you, as an individual, may be great.

9

BEHIND THE SCENES

Experiences, or opinions based on experiences, of an arbitrary cross section of artists working within a theatrical community can provide insights concerning the state of that community, its weak - nesses and its strengths. Such insights may be helpful to other artists who are thinking about coming to the community to work and live.

In this chapter I have asked a random number of actors, directors, playwrights and designers to express their views about San Francisco theatre as candidly as possible. Many have been quite willing to be identified. Others have voiced reluctance, believing that they could not afford, for a variety of reasons, to express them - selves as honestly as they would like unless they were permitted to remain anonymous. (This fact alone may have some significance.) I am convinced, however, that the opinions of these latter people are representative and valuable, so I have included their statements here and have honored their requests to stay unrecognized.

Following are brief biographies of the artists who gave per - mission to be identified:

HOPE ALEXANDER-WILLIS began her acting career with the **Actor's Workshop** at the age of fifteen. She has done television and film work, played leading roles with **A.C.T.** and has recently been under contract to the **Berkeley Repertory Theatre**. ALMA BECKER lived in the Bay area for a decade, acting and directing at various small theatres. She is the recipient of two directing awards from the **Bay Area Theatre Critics Circle**. She now lives and works in New York. STEVE COATS was born in the Bay area and practiced theatre here for a dozen years, acting chiefly at the **Eureka Theatre**. He, too, now lives in New York. CAB COVAY is an actor-sound designer, stage manager and sometime director who has worked in radio, films and television as well as local theatre. He has been in the Bay area for the past thirty years. DANIEL CURZON is a published novelist and a playwright whose plays have been produced at **Theatre Rhinoceros**, the **San Francisco Repertory** and the **One Act Theatre**. ANDREW DE SHONG, a set designer, has practiced his craft in the Bay area for more than fifteen years. His sets have graced the stages of such diverse companies as the **Eureka** and the **Lamplighters** in San Francisco. JIM HAYNIE acted here for about eight years, most notably in *True West* at the **Magic Theatre**. He now works in television and films. KENNA HUNT came to the Bay area in 1963 and has appeared with many of the local companies, including the **Eureka**, the **Magic**, the **One Act**, the **Julian** and the **San Francisco Repertory**. Her most recent **Equity** work was with the **San Jose Repertory**. IRVING ISRAEL, an actor with the **Berkeley Repertory** for the past few years, was with the **Actor's Workshop** for seven years, produced plays for his own **Venture Theatre**, and has also acted with the **San Francisco Repertory** and the **One Act Theatre**. JULIAN LOPEZ-MORILLAS has been working in Bay area theatre now for almost fifteen years. His San Francisco appearances have been mostly with the **Eureka**, the **Magic** and the **Julian**. NANCY MORRISON performed locally as an actress off and on for ten years. She is now an employee of **Cannon Films** in Hollywood. MARK MURPHEY is an actor who has worked exclusively for **A.C.T.** for close to eight years. JOHN O'KEEFE is a playwright and director who has been in the Bay area since 1972. His play *All Night Long*, produced at the **Magic Theatre** in 1980, received several critical awards. ADELE PROOM was an actress with the **One Act Theatre** in its early

118

days. She now acts with other theatres in the Bay area. GAEL RUSSELL is a costume designer who started work here in 1979. She has designed and coordinated costumes for the **Eureka** and the **Actors' Ark**, among other theatres. SYDNEY WALKER worked with the **Interplayers** and the **Playhouse** in the early 1950s, left to pursue a career in New York, returned to act with **A.C.T.** in 1974 and was a member of that company through the 1984-'85 season.

ON CAREER PROBLEMS

WILLIS: There is always the problem of having only two or three Equity houses in which to work. I've never had a job outside the theatre. (Knock on wood.)

ANON.: When I audition for a role in a play, even in a small theatre, I don't appreciate being told that to get the part or to join the company I must agree to spend so many hours a week doing other work. I know someone has to staff the box-office and clean the rest rooms, but that is not the kind of job for which I'm applying.

BECKER: Where's the audience? Where are the theatre administrators? In waiver houses the director is often expected to act as producer and janitor as well.

COATS: Lack of money and jobs is a tremendous frustration. I find that it is much harder for directors to develop their skills here than actors.

COVAY: Actors, who would seem to be the least expendable portion of the show, are actually the most. They are footlight fodder, at the mercy of whoever pays the rent. Money or the lack of it influences every decision, artistic or otherwise. Socially, it is a life of derision.

ANON.: I'm appalled at the way auditions are held. In the old days you were just asked to read from a script. Now, even to get a part in a small theatre where they won't pay you a dime, you're expected to give the director a photo (which has cost you five dollars for the copy) and a professional-looking resume (which is laborious to prepare or costly to have done by somebody else) and you're supposed to have two or three prepared pieces to present. Somebody told me that at one theatre the director asks you to tell him a joke. My God, I'm an actress, not a joke teller!

CURZON: Theatres will do works about other minorities without blinking, but they still think (mistakenly) that only gays will watch plays about gays. I

119

consider this old-fashioned and narrow-minded, particularly since I write works that are not bound by political categories.

DE SHONG: I can't think of a single designer who makes his living by exclusively designing in the Bay area. (Other problems include lack of ade - quate technical help in executing sets, lack of budget, sometimes incom - petent production management, selection of designers by nepotism, unin - formed judgment or bizarre competition, lack of any coherent, formulated aesthetic for design: in short—the same things found anywhere.)

HAYNIE: Lack of expertise in directing, producing areas. I think this leads to leakage of real power to the big two (L.A. and N.Y.).

HUNT: In New York, both paying jobs and showcases can lead to another paying job, either by being seen or through an agent. The Bay area has no (such) agents, really—agents who, once having recognized your talent, at - tempt to find paying jobs for you.

ANON.: Too few directors here have any real respect for actors and acting as an art. Some do, but most do not. One director in an interview said she didn't like to work with actors who were "too confident." Another director said on television that if an actor came to him with any pre-conceived ideas about how to play a part, he wouldn't hire that actor. He said he liked an actor to be a "blank page" on which he (the director) could write whatever he wanted. Well, I'm a professional with years of training and experience. I'm not arrogant and I will take direction, but I do have some confidence in my own ability and I do have ideas of my own. I am not a blank page, for God's sake!

ISRAEL: Just as the world has changed, so has the theatre—and it may never recover from what has happened to it.

LOPEZ-MORILLAS: Principally, lack of Equity work. Also lack of good direc - tors. Sometimes, when I work as a director (esp. in Shakespeare) lack of technique in actors' training.

MORRISON: The dearth of Equity production is disheartening, to say the least. Secondly, in reference to the waiver house situation, it is amazing to me that people with minimal talent end up as directors and artistic directors.

MURPHEY: I am fortunate along those lines in that I have a good job with good pay in a good company. Most of my frustrations are for my fellow actors who suffer from the hands of rather merciless management in other Bay area theatre companies.

O'KEEFE: I'm heartbroken and very depressed about the state of the theatre here. It is getting more and more conservative. It's frustrating that foun -

dations won't give individual grants to artists. The money given out should serve the artist, not just to help an artist serve a particular theatre.

PROOM: There is a small amount of work for an Equity actress like myself. Open casting is too often not really open.

RUSSELL: There's a lack of respect for artists by theatre boards, a general dis - interest in costumes and how they are produced. This includes money allo - cated and money received.

ANON.: I get Equity jobs every season or so, and I've got acting credits up the kazoo. But the waiver houses never call me to read for a role, even though I might be exactly right for the part. Yes, I know they have open audi - tions, but I won't go to cattle calls. You can say I'm too proud, if you want, but I've paid my dues and I think an experienced professional is en - titled to a little more deferential treatment than if he'd just graduated from drama school. The younger directors working on the local scene now seem threatened by experienced actors, as if afraid we'll be difficult, and I think that's very sad. I'm available, but I'm not used as much as I should be.

WALKER: I have earned my living as an actor since 1955. I have no frus - trations, so long as I am under contract to A.C.T.

ON CURRENT BAY AREA THEATRE

WILLIS: It ranges from the sublime to the ridiculous. We have a large range of theatre here, from what I call the "pee-pee-ca-ca" school to the sterile "look-at-our-sets-and-costumes-aren't-we-pretty" ones, and everything in-between! I think the Bay area has some of the most gifted people in the United States trying to work in it. Too bad they can't get more support.

ANON.: Once in a while there's a really top-notch show done here, when everything blends—the acting, directing, designs, sound, etc. This is won - derful when it happens. Too often, though, even in the productions which are most successful, there are weak performances, the set is shabby or something else is wrong. Due to nepotism or other personal reasons, the directors and producers do not really make an effort to get the absolute top talent available—they will have three or four good artists in their company and they will settle for lovers, friends, etc. who are not so good—or cast someone to pay off a debt. Maybe he's helped to build the sets or some - thing, and they want to compensate him, so they give him a role. This keeps the production from achieving full professional quality.

BECKER: Quality varies theatre to theatre, production to production. We are a community strong in actors and designers. We are short on good directors.

The current trend to slick productions threatens the foundation that has moved San Francisco theatre at least this far: the sense of risk, not playing safe in either choice of play or production values. I am not interested in predigested theatre.

COATS: San Francisco theatre is comparable to theatre anywhere else. Good work is good work no matter where it comes from; bad work is bad work. It is really sort of pointless in my mind to compare or compete with other theatres. By denigrating New York theatre, we are not improving San Francisco theatre.

CURZON: I think there is a great deal of good theatre here, more than any one person can possibly absorb.

DE SHONG: Good and bad theatre exists in some proportion everywhere. Today San Francisco is a very fertile area for new playwrights and that's exactly as it should be. The other arts will develop from the emphasis on the pro - duction of new plays. It's pretty sad when you have the other extreme: wildly innovative design, marvellous acting of classic theatre pieces, and no new plays. On the other hand, San Francisco is in danger of becoming insular and more provincial perpetually. . . . There is a real tendency to forget or ignore true standards of excellence.

HAYNIE: [The theatre here] is slowly improving in quality, but we'll go faster when more people spend more time doing it. We're on the edge of real growth.

HUNT: I think it [the quality of theatre here] is quite high, as a matter of fact. The percentage of theatre, well-acted, in the ninety-nine seat houses is higher than all the off-Broadway stuff I used to see in New York.

ISRAEL: In my opinion there is, generally speaking, a great lack of "quality" theatre here. And for that matter, I suspect that the theatre everywhere in America has deteriorated greatly.

LOPEZ-MORILLAS: [There is] good acting in the more established theatres; originality and courage to experiment with new writing and new forms; strong commitment to artistic quality by local theatre workers; technical and design values are not up to the level of acting except in the more es - tablished companies; a general ignorance of what good directing is and little understanding of what the director contributes.

ANON.: With the exception of A.C.T., the local theatres (most of them) have become playwrights' theatres. I'm not saying this is right or wrong, good or bad. But the emphasis in the productions is on seeing how the play works and perhaps promoting the play for publication or production else - where. Little concern is expressed for the actors or the acting. This is unfortunate, because if the acting is better, isn't the play going to look better?

MURPHEY: From what I have seen the quality is proportional to the number of professional people (actors) hired for the job. There might be a few excep - tions, but on the whole this is true. The road companies that come here may be the exceptions. ˜

O'KEEFE: I think the quality of theatre here is very good. But then, I don't see a lot. I'm more interested in making theatre than going to the theatre. There's real talent here. What the Snake Theatre has done is very impor - tant. Some of the theatre produced here has no point of view.

ANON.: It's great that so many new plays are being produced here, but the *kinds* of plays being produced are beginning to upset me. The emphasis on "new forms" is now so strong that almost anything abstract is con - sidered worth doing—when it isn't, always. Some of the "experimental" works are really bummers. Crashing bores, as a matter of fact. And I think a lot of local actors and theatregoers agree with this and wouldn't mind at all seeing some new plays being produced which were traditional in form—but where are they? Modern playwrights are being discouraged from writing realistic plays because the theatre managers aren't interested in them. They *are* producing some plays that are more trivial (if you look beneath the form) than a lot of the plays they're probably turning down. Nobody is benefiting from this situation, least of all the playgoer. The managers are simply being self-indulgent, involving themselves in a kind of intellectual masturbation—giving pleasure to no one but themselves.

PROOM: Both the choice of material and the acting talent range from the very, very good to the bottom of the barrel.

WALKER: Good—bad—indifferent. No better or worse than in New York, Chi - cago, Washington, D.C., Seattle, Boston.

ON CRITICS

WILLIS: As an actor, of course, I'm always pleased to see nice things connected to my work, but I never take reviews seriously. When I was at A.C.T. I had an experience that changed my view of critics forever. There was an actor there—his name was Nick Courtland—who I had the misfortune to be cast opposite in *Tiny Alice.* Now this actor, and it upsets me to even use that word connected to him, was not only a non-talent. He was the anti-unicorn, a black hole in space. The kind of actor who would jump acts in the middle of scenes, forget lines and cues, try to upstage every - body, be rude and unprofessional, you name it, the works! I had never in

123

all my experience worked with anyone that talentless as a performer, or odious as a human. When we opened, one of the top critics in S.F. gave him a rave review, much to the amazement of all involved. I realized then and there that I could never take another review seriously, and to this day I haven't.

ANON.: The critics here are okay—as good as anywhere, I guess. My main complaint against them is that they don't seem to really know much about acting, different styles of acting, that different plays *require* different styles, etc. When they evaluate a show they've seen, they can't seem to separate the writing, the directing and the acting. If they like a play or a director, for example, then they give the production a good review. If they don't care for a play, then no matter how well it's done they aren't sympa - thetic to the work of the actor and the director. They're not very discerning in that respect.

BECKER: It depends on how I feel about the work. When I know there is a problem or weakness in a production and a reviewer sees that but also sees the positive, that's easier to accept. When a reviewer understands and ana - lyzes the reasons for understanding, that is an exciting review—then you have transferred your vision to the other person. When a reviewer has a preconceived idea of the "right" way to do a play, that is usually a review to avoid reading.

COATS: It took me a long time to learn to ignore [the critics]. I urge artists to read criticism carefully or not at all. Both good and bad criticism is always "after the fact," and while theatre is alive and changes constantly, the act of documenting a review is fixed and deadening. . . . Both good and bad reviews can be problematic. Best to leave them in a time capsule to be opened ten years after the show is over. Or twenty.

COVAY: I like critics. They are, after all, audience members. Concerning what they write, it is not quality that counts, but quantity. Some of them know what they're talking about, many of them don't. Few have shared my experience of making a living at [the theatre]. How do they know? I have been praised and blamed for equally uninformed reasons.

CURZON: When critics review me unfavorably, which has happened only with one work, I try to see if they are correct. If they are, I'll try to adjust the work. If they are wrong-headed or off-target, I simply forget about them. (Not before considering bombing their homes, of course.)

ANON.: There is one Bay area actor to whom the critics in the Bay area always give favorable reviews; he is their fair-haired boy. They call him brilliant, highly talented, and generally can't give him enough praise. Other actors who have worked with this man know that he's a bag of tricks—he's a solo performer, doesn't play with his fellow performers (doesn't listen) and

124

is a conscious scene-stealer—he'll do anything onstage to keep the atten - tion on himself, even when the focus belongs elsewhere. Some directors are awed by him and don't even try to control him. You can't respect the critics who praise this actor and can't see how dishonest he is. . . . The sad thing is, the man does have talent, but he has been permitted to get away with murder because the critics never criticize him for the things for which he should be criticized. In this case, then, by giving an actor such rave reviews they are doing both the actor and our theatre a disfavor. He will never change his ways, and the theatre must suffer his outrageous perform - ing—because the critics champion it as being "brilliant" and "sensitive." What it is, actually, is selfish and insular.

DE SHONG: After entertaining the usual aggressive phantasies, I admit there's usually a reason for the negative remark. Often the personalities, eco - nomics and logistics aren't apparent, but the critical comment could be anticipated. Sets don't improve after opening night (actors often do), so constructive criticism is usually hindsight that can possibly be applied to the next production. Critics in the Bay area have some impact, mostly negative, with the public and the box office. Good reviews don't get jobs or even maintain them. Theatre workers here seem to be convinced that critics are unqualified boors. The same theatre workers don't see more than a few productions outside their own theatres. Although I'm fairly active as audience, most conscientious critics see three times the number of produc - tions I do in a year. Considering this, their judgments do have some im - portance for me.

HAYNIE: I listen to see what they saw. Usually they're honest, though preju - diced in some way, but that's part of the message. If you're really doing a good job it's hard for them not to say so. Also, I do pray that reviewers take anti-pomposity pills regularly and avoid trashing a whole show for the sake of one item—have a sense of proportion.

HUNT: I read all critical reviews of my work and am naturally affected, but I try to take *all* reviews (negative and positive) with a grain of salt. "One man's meat, etc."

ISRAEL: It would be silly for any actor to concern himself or herself with any opinions of any critics. An actor learns after a little experience, to trust himself. I think it's too difficult to say how I would respond to critics "in general." I can respond to critics only specifically. I rarely receive bad reviews.

ANON.: A few local critics go out of their way to be supportive of experi - mental theatre, and that's good in one sense. But sometimes these critics lose all sense of proportion in the matter. A couple of years ago the *Chronicle* critic reviewed a show that was done in a garage somewhere in Noe Valley. He thought it was great—in his review he said it was bril -

125

liant, a riveting theatrical experience. Long pauses with no dialogue were compelling, he said. Even the noise filtering into the garage from outside in the street, he claimed, added to the excitement of the evening. More drivel like that. A friend of mine remarked that maybe if the critic had gone out *into* the street and been mugged, it would have made the "rivet -ing theatrical experience" complete for him.

LOPEZ-MORILLAS: I feel I can decide for myself whether a critic has a legiti -mate beef or whether he's just carping or has misunderstood the work. Of course, it's never fun being trashed. Principally, I realize that in a town short on competent PR and advertising, a couple of major reviews (esp. the *Chronicle*) can make or break a show. A bad *Chronicle* review always hurts, at the box office more than personally.

MORRISON: When reviews are unfavorable I remind myself that it's one man's (woman's) opinion. Of course, when they are favorable I admire their perspicacity and sensitivity. . . . I have finally learned not to take things too personally. One critic is notorious for falling asleep immedi -ately after arrival. The standing joke is that loud snoring indicates a bad review, although it could also mean a rave if accompanied by heavy breathing.

O'KEEFE: I'm not a review reader, but I'm not against reviewers. Critics need to be there, and they do keep some people in line. Perhaps the critics have too much power, if they can decide whether or not a show is to be suc -cessful. Sometimes their focus on the art of a production is missing in their reviews.

ANON.: I have received reviews which proclaimed me an absolute genius. Also, about six years ago, a new critic in town reviewed me and declared that I was the weakest member of that show's cast. I didn't believe him, and I don't believe the critics who have called me a genius, either.

PROOM: Nobody likes a bad review and I am no exception. I always hope that the critics who see my performances come with an open mind, leaving their likes and dislikes for this kind of theatre or that kind of theatre at the front door. . . . The good critic whose cause is to help theatre advance and build audiences, I listen to and value his (her) constructive criticism. . . . Then there are the critics whose opinions and how they look in print are more important than the play they're reviewing, and these critics are of little value to me.

RUSSELL: Any review is a good review if it accurately reflects the work. Crit -ics need to be firmer, or better, tough in their opinions. Too much not-so-good stuff gets favorable response.

ANON.: Many critics in the Bay area are very provincial, very "little theatre" in their attitudes, and in some instances even hostile towards more traditional commercial theatre. This makes it hard for those of us who want to make a living in the theatre and who genuinely like traditional theatre—i.e., mu - sicals, light comedies or realistic dramas. The critics aren't supportive of these kinds of projects.

WALKER: As we work on plays or roles for five or six weeks, daily, before critics see us, I must assume we know what we are about more than any critic who sees us for one performance in a given part.

COMPARING PAST AND PRESENT

WILLIS: There is much more theatre here now than when I was a kid. It seems to me, though, that there are fewer independent Equity shows that come and cast here. That's a shame. San Francisco could be such a great theatre town. But hopefully that will grow as more of the smaller professional houses get more support—and by professional, by the way, I mean it in the real sense of the word, not the monetary one!

ANON.: There's much more theatre here now than there was twenty years ago, but I don't know that it's necessarily much better. One thing I do know: actors aren't paid any better, in some cases not as well. At $10 a perfor - mance under a special Equity agreement, I made $60 a week with the Ac - tor's Workshop, playing at both the Marines Memorial and the Encore in 1960-'61-'62. That's the equivalent of at least $300 a week today, and maybe more in the 80s money market. A free lance actor playing at the Magic, the Eureka or the One Act Theatre Company in 1986 would never receive that much—and these theatres have bigger box-office receipts and more grant money from foundations than the Workshop ever did.

BECKER: I think there's more gossip and rumour, and more overt use of power.

COATS: Yes, there is [growth]. Theatre Communications [Center of the Bay Area] is a good thing, BATWA [Bay Area Theatre Workers Associaton] is a good thing. The emerging grants given in the last few years to small theatres is a good thing, and it is about to be destroyed by the Reagan administration. On the other hand, the small theatres are trying to become slick, and they are losing their grip. Too often small theatres here become insular, almost incestuous. It is too easy for some small theatres to be - come the "exclusive" clubhouse of either a group or a company, at the ex - clusion of the outside world.

COVAY: There has been some development in *me* these last twenty years or so, so it's hard for me to tell if there's more activity in the theatre or if I'm just getting paid more—could be both.

CURZON: I think theatre has burgeoned greatly in the years I've been here. There's just a whole lot *more*.

DE SHONG: Comparing 1986 to 1976, there have been vast improvements: far greater audience development, fewer imitative-echo productions from else - where, more companies, more paid theatre workers, more conscientious critics, an extraordinary emphasis on new plays and playwrights.

ANON.: Non-profit theatres receive grant money to help them keep their doors open today. In the 50s and 60s we depended solely on box-office receipts. Nobody was subsidizing us. The grants relieve today's managers and artis - tic directors of a lot of anxiety, and that's probably good. On the other hand, being more financially secure—it's like being on welfare—there's a tendency to become lazy, more self-indulgent, and maybe to do more plays which the *directors* want to do rather than plays which audiences want to see.

HAYNIE: I don't think anyone has shown the vigor of the Actor's Workshop for a while, onstage anyway. Satire seems flaccid these days, but the inti - mate theatre is very hearty. I see a feedbed for a very healthy future growth.

HUNT: Yes [there has been growth]. I believe the community of theatre has grown quite a bit. When I first came here, there were no workshop or ninety-nine seat productions and few contract opportunities. Now at least one can practice.

ISRAEL: I was fortunate enough to belong to one of the best theatrical com - panies in America. [The Actor's Workshop] was an important company because it understood deeply what theatre was and what its purposes were. . . . Directors, actors, set designers and lighting technicians were all dedicated to try to produce greatness in every respect. . . . Many things have happened since that particular theatre company passed out of existence. . . . There are still some people in this area who are trying and often-times succeeding in producing quality theatre. But quality is not at all consistent. We are not hearing from as many great playwrights as pre - viously. There are a few but not enough. Also there are now very few out - standing directors. And in the acting field, mediocrity abounds and is readily accepted by audiences as fine work.

LOPEZ-MORILLAS: It seems to me there's somewhat more quality work across the board, especially at the waiver-house level, but the difference isn't dramatic. More theatres are paying actors more, which is a very good

128

sign. One thing that seems to remain fairly constant is a healthy (?) inde - pendence from commercialism.

MORRISON: I believe there are more theatres than there were ten years ago, and that the ninety-nine seat houses are taken much more seriously than they were in the 60s. This is a very healthy development. On the negative side, I do not believe there has been concomitant growth in aesthetic quality or vision. It is extremely rare to leave the theatre satiated, exhila - rated, scintillated or enraptured.

MURPHEY: In the years I have been here I feel the public has become more aware of theatre. The smaller theatres profiting from the waiver have grown in size though not enough in benevolence toward actors. I haven't really seen enough to say more.

O'KEEFE: The work in theatre here is growing more and more conservative; people are feeling the Reagan crunch. There is a lot of trying to make peo - ple think what they're doing is new, when it isn't. We should be opening new horizons of theatre for the next generation. But if you try to do this, by the time you are accepted and recognized, there has been too much dues paying. Five years ago there was more experimental theatre, I think. There is a scarcity of spaces in which to perform now.

ANON.: We live today in a society that is filled with chaos. Our local theatre reflects that society, not only in the plays which the waiver theatres choose to do but in the way the young people now approach the theatrical arts—playwriting, acting, etc. Irreverence is the order of the day. Well con - structed plays are considered banal, directors who are solid craftsmen are called "unimaginative," disciplined acting is derided as sterile. Tried and true standards (no matter if they were good enough for the ancient Greek playwrights and the greatest actors who have ever lived!) are mocked; they exist in the 1980s only to be demolished. I'm not saying that the theatre of twenty years ago was perfect, God knows it wasn't! But it seems to me that critics then were able to recognize and appreciate professional skill. Today they don't. An actor who gives a polished performance is put down as "mannered." Erratic, uneven, improvised and unthought-out acting is applauded as "richly creative." It's disgraceful. Sorry—but in my opinion it's a terrible state of affairs.

PROOM: In the early 60s the theatrical community was less developed and company oriented. We have grown in numbers of theatres and with the advent of grant money we've seen business staffs arise and monies spent on a more commercial approach to building audience. I think today's theatre is beginning to recognize that theatre is a business and the more professional actors they have on their stage the more chances of success.

WALKER: Cannot comment. Not sufficient first-hand knowledge.

129

SUGGESTIONS FOR IMPROVEMENT

WILLIS: It's a matter of community support. I also think that various theatres should form more of an alliance with each other . . . pool our talents, as it were. I think there should be more professional courtesies extended, not just from the smaller houses to the larger houses but from the larger thea - tres, too. . . . I know that a lot of the actors that work in the smaller houses tend to bad-mouth A.C.T. or B.R.T. [Berkeley Repertory The - atre] . . . I think that's stupid. We are all on the same road, we are artists. *Les Enfants du Paradis*! We should be trying to find ways to help the whole of us.

ANON.: Directors should use much more objectivity in their casting. They should not put people in demanding roles merely because they're friends, lovers, or because they worked the box-office on the last show. One di - rector lowered the age of a character twenty years in a play she directed, just so she could cast an actor who was a friend and whom she particularly liked. The critics didn't notice the difference, but people who knew the play knew what she'd done. It wasn't right.

BECKER: My hope is that the San Francisco theatre community will draw on people who will continue to strive, risk, and be responsible communica - tions artists. Less compromise.

COATS: Write letters of support to the California Arts Council. Many, many, many of us depend on grants on the local and national level, so we must write the politicians and tell them how our lives are on the line. Write let - ters to editors of newspapers, write directors of television and radio to en - large their coverage. If you are an actor working in a ninety-nine seat the - atre, realize that you have no rights unless you demand them. Theatres are built on the talents of their actors and technicians. Actors and technical people have power; they must not be slaves to theatres that pay everybody *but* the actors and techs. Stay angry; something may be done if enough people want it.

COVAY: Conditions would be mightily improved around here if two-thirds of the theatre artists I know would move to Peoria, though I doubt if this im - provement will be realized.

CURZON: We need more and better and cheaper spaces to use for theatres. Rip-off property owners should be sent packing. The city of San Francisco should provide a half dozen theatre spaces for little theatres, instead of *everything* for mainstream shows.

ANON.: There is a strong need for the local managers to develop a sense of business ethics in dealing with performers. Promises are easily made and just as easily broken in waiver houses where there is no contract. But pro ducers should know that the word does get around about them when they are unfair with actors. In some Equity companies, actors have been asked to "kick back" their salaries and then not cast again if they refused to do so. This is dirty pool—and managers should learn that it's no way to play the game. There are things which are morally right and morally wrong, even in the theatre.

DE SHONG: It's pretty clear that local, state and national governments are go ing to avoid their responsibility to fund the arts. That leaves corporations and individuals. I'm not optimistic.

HAYNIE: Non-profit theatres should have a league, improving communications between themselves to solve production problems and to plan professional productions, thereby providing local professional growth. Together with professional groups such as the unions, they could discover the means to realize a greater potential.

HUNT: Arrange so that actors can be paid. This way there would be fewer cliques, etc. They would want best actors to be *found*, if they were paying money. (Of course "arranging" this is easier said than done.)

ISRAEL: I'm not at all sure that conditions can or will improve for thespians here in San Francisco. Lightning rarely strikes twice in the same place. But the artistic community should find the great directors and then give them their dedication and their monetary support so that they can give what they have to give to the community! Such things will not happen in my lifetime.

ANON.: Directors should consider it a part of their job to go to other theatres and see what kind of work is being done elsewhere. This would also give them a chance to see new actors—giving a finished performance, not just an audition piece. . . . I was in a play a few months ago which attracted a lot of attention and had good reviews. Only one director that I know of came to see it, and that was because she was a close personal friend. That's disgraceful! I know that the more prominent directors are busy people, but I still think they should make more of an effort to get around to see the work at other theatres.

LOPEZ-MORILLAS: Actors should organize for better pay and working con ditions—that is to say, to demand more respect for their craft. Theatres should cooperate with Equity on long-term plans to employ union actors contractually, possibly under a middle agreement between the present LORT and guest artist arrangements and the waiver-house rules, to ease the transition to full Equity status. . . . The formation of BATWA is an important step toward the first goal. Greater flexibility by the board of Equity and a cooperative effort by both artists and management in the smaller theatres will be necessary for the second.

MORRISON: I would love to see more Equity shows mounted here, more inde-pendent producers willing to take risks on new material, more art commis-sion money earmarked for established waiver houses with a stipulation that wages for actors be a high priority budget item.

MURPHEY: I feel conditions could be improved if the managers and producers of the smaller theatres (particularly waiver houses) used some of their money to pay actors. The real problems for the actor here are pay and jobs. Working conditions could be improved, I'm sure, but money comes first. More theatres, more jobs, more pay.

ANON.: Better work discipline. That's what's needed, especially in the waiver houses. I've had so many bad experiences in disorganized productions that I just won't accept roles in any but top companies anymore. . . . Profes-sionalism is a state of mind, an attitude, a way of approaching your work. It's having your act together. As an older actress, it makes me sad to see so many talented younger people behaving erratically, conducting them-selves without discipline in rehearsal and performance. I hope the new crop of directors and producers will realize that they are the role models. They must set the standards—and first, they must recognize that standards *exist*, before they can be established.

O'KEEFE: I would like to see much more controversy on the local theatre scene. The theatres should take more chances. We must have explora-tion—the drek and gook must go! We *have* to discover new things. . . . Actors should be treated with more respect. Managers and directors treat them atrociously now. (I've heard the way they talk about them!)

PROOM: When theatres start out, actors are often asked to build sets, take tickets, sell coffee and do clean-up jobs as well as act. As the theatres be-come more profitable, in many instances, actors are still required to per-form these non-acting functions. The last people to share in the profits of the theatres are the actors—who often wait in line behind janitors, electricians, p.r. people, musicians and, of course, directors. The lot of the actor and the theatres would be improved if the actors were given their fair share. . . . [This will happen] if the actors realize their own value and do something about it.

ANON.: In his book *Journey to the Center of the Theatre*, Walter Kerr says that while we undoubtedly have profited from the vogue of the avant-garde and the theatre of the absurd, we may very well have lost an entire generation of potential dramatists in process. As a realistic playwright living in the Bay area, I couldn't agree more. Experimental theatre is fine, but there are

132

still important things which can, and should, be said in traditional forms. You'd never know this, though, from the kinds of plays which some of our small theatres consistently produce. It's as if they think that abstract works were the only kind of play to be taken seriously! The pendulum needs to swing back a little bit. After all, abstract or symbolic plays aren't always profound, and traditional plays aren't always trivial. We need a greater balance between traditional plays and new experimental plays. As Walter Kerr put it, many a potential realistic dramatist has been left crippled because of the vogue of the avant-garde. This situation needs to be changed—before the avant-garde plays themselves become traditional!

RUSSELL: We need contracts, of course, which we don't always get. We need a costumers' co-op for resources, job listings, and worker availability.

WALKER: There needs to be more theatre here, more performances, and more audience interest. I can only hope [that some of these things will happen].

ANON.: Since actors get little or no money for their work in local theatre, how about compensating for this with more personal publicity or billing? If producers were willing to help *build* local feature players, if not "stars," the public—which acquires favorite performers—would respond when a certain actor was highly publicized as a member of the cast. . . . This will only happen when managers and directors recognize the value of having highly trained and experienced actors in their shows. Right now, they're indifferent. They consider actors a dime a dozen. But actors can make or break even a good script. . . . Polished actors, of course, make it.

ADVICE TO POTENTIAL NEWCOMERS

WILLIS: Good luck.

ANON.: The Bay area is a charming and wonderful place to live. But it is no place to build a professional career as an actor, director or technician. You can go so far here and no farther. You can build a good artistic reputation and win Critics Circle awards, but those things won't help you one whit in negotiating a better salary for yourself. And no matter what your track record, if you ask for billing, whether it's in a waiver house or a full Equity production, the managers are shocked. They'll accuse you of being on an ego trip and they'll say that you've got rocks in your head even to suggest such a thing. They do not *think* professionally. So just be pre - pared for what you're getting into if you decide to come here.

COVAY: I couldn't honestly recommend this place to an outsider contempla - ting a career in theatre because they will soon be forced to move on to

L.A. or N.Y.C. It's a real effort to hang on here—if I were less versatile I couldn't do it myself, and I'm a native.

CURZON: Theatre people coming here from elsewhere need to know that it *does* matter who you know, as in any theatrical environment. Contact with directors and producers leads to production of your work far more than simply submission of scripts.

ANON.: Come ahead! Maybe you'll be the genius to turn the whole theatre scene here around.

DE SHONG: Five years ago San Francisco was a good place for young actors and designers who were looking for experience and not too concerned with making a living. There hasn't been a normal turn-over; the same personnel are still here and forming closed companies.

HAYNIE: Invest a little more time—re-enlist in the war on poverty, get a job. But, be enthusiastic.

HUNT: If [you] want a break from "hack" or commercial type stuff and really want to "create" for a while without pay, come. But don't expect to make a living yet.

ISRAEL: I don't think I'd care to "advise" anyone on this subject. Every person must find his own way as best he can. San Francisco is probably the best place to live in the United States.

ANON.: Well, I've worked more steadily than other actresses and have had a good share of the Equity contracts offered here. But I'm leaving to try New York. What does that tell you?

LOPEZ-MORILLAS: Don't expect to make a living wage until you've been here long enough to establish yourself and make connections—unless you have a side-line like voice work or heavy commercial potential (even then it'll take a while). Don't come at all if your principal objectives are fame and bucks, or film and TV. If you want to do good work in the theatre with good people for not-great money and recognition, this is the place for you.

MORRISON: Don't come unless you have a second skill to depend upon for survival.

MURPHEY: My advice would be, if you want to earn a living, either work at A.C.T., Berkeley Rep, or a regular job. Otherwise, look elsewhere. If you can do film work, go to New York or L.A.

O'KEEFE: I've changed my tune on this subject lately. I used to tell people to come here, but now I can't tell anyone he'd do very well. If you come here to work solely in the theatre, you're going to be broke.

ANON.: San Francisco has a reputation for being a great theatre town, and ac - tors on full Equity contracts playing a six week run at the Curran Theatre can have a ball here. But it's a different story if you plan to live here and work in shows that originate in the Bay area. Think twice before you de - cide to try it. Then think again.

PROOM: Keep going!

RUSSELL: Persistence, guts—be a nudge, go and get it!

WALKER: Don't come unless you have a firm job offer—preferably from A.C.T.

    In studying this cross section of opinion, one becomes aware of ambiguities, controversial attitudes and, in some cases, remark - able similarities of notions and ideas. This is not a scientific survey, of course, and no absolute conclusions can be drawn from the answers given by the persons interviewed. Still, out of the mass of information which these particular artists have divulged, questions arise and a few points seem clear.
    One of the ills of modern San Francisco theatre, in my opinion, is reflected in Nancy Morrison's expression of dismay over how people of minimal talent are suddenly placed in positions of administrative power. In fact, this may be the root of *all* trouble with San Francisco theatre. As editors and publishers do not seek out genuinely qualified people to work as critics on the *Chron - icle* and the *Examiner* (not to mention the smaller papers) so, it seems, theatre boards of directors opt to appoint somebody's best friend as a company's artistic director. Or they opt to appoint some neophyte to the top position, as opposed to a person with an extensive background, because the neophyte will bring, they think, a fresh, contemporary approach to the company's work. Yes, the Peter Principle is as visible in the world of San Francisco theatre as it is in the world of commerce, and if it doesn't breed outright dis - aster it does breed a continuance of mediocrity.
    One does not become a professonal in the theatre, or in any other art or science, simply by announcing the fact. It takes more

than talent, ideals and a burning desire; those are the things, hope - fully, one has for starters. Becoming a real professional requires a period of gestation; it is not something one achieves simply by snapping one's fingers or hanging up a sign in the window. Yet the Mickey Rooney-Judy Garland syndrome of "Hey, kids, let's put on a show" still flourishes in San Francisco. I won't say that's alto - gether a bad thing. We all feel a certain sympathy and benevolent affection for young talent as it struggles to express itself. The people who founded the **Magic Theatre**, the **Eureka** and the **One Act** were brave souls, and bless them for accomplishing what they did. But if the founders of these companies had worked with other, more established companies, and if they had analyzed those companies' successes and failures, think how much better qualified they would have been when they started their own theatres! Much of the struggles which they went through, and much of the learning process they are still going through, would have been made much easier before they set themselves up as administrators and directors.

Professionalism is an attitude gained through extensive knowl - edge and experience, and one does not gain that knowledge and experience through working solely with one's peers. Actors and directors who really want to grow will seek opportunities to work with people more experienced than themselves, in order to learn from them (even if they learn what *not* to do!). Unfortunately, according to my observations, most San Francisco directors, and perhaps some actors, are more comfortable working with people on a *lower* level of development than themselves than with more experienced artists. The neophyte director, to a certain degree insecure and covetous of his or her position and power, casts actors who are easy to control. These are usually his friends or those in his peer group, and thus the Peter Principle continues in effect. Many good actors work, but the most experienced and qualified people do not necessarily get the jobs.

In an article in the *Bay Guardian* issue of March 12th, 1986, Misha Berson (a woman of admirable chutzpah but limited pro - fessional theatre background) joins her good friend and colleague Bernard Weiner of the *Chronicle* to write about William Ball's "fall" and to give us what she calls "a prescription for what ails A.C.T." She criticizes the company for its choice of plays and its casting mis - takes. Does she mean to imply that these faults, if they are faults, are indigenous only to **A.C.T.**? She's never seen a poor play at the

Eureka, the **Magic** or the **Julian** or the **One Act Theatre**? Every role in these theatres is cast with the best actor available? I think she knows very well that every theatre company makes the same kinds of mistakes, but like Weiner she will never write an article criticizing one of the smaller companies but relishes every opportunity to blast away at **A.C.T.** She asks why **A.C.T.** doesn't use some of the more established players from the smaller theatres. She has forgot-ten, apparently, if indeed she ever knew, that Sydney Walker, Marrian Walters, Drew Eshelman and several others, including my-self, acted in other San Francisco theatres before being hired by **A.C.T.** I think her suggestion is a good one, but it should work both ways. Why don't the **Eureka**, the **Magic** and the **One Act**, for instance, use **A.C.T.** actors? I know several very good actors who have worked in San Francisco for years but have never been asked to play a role at any of these theatres. Insular casting and nep-otism, with best friends and wives and lovers getting the best parts, exist at the **Eureka** and the **Magic** every bit as much as they have existed at **A.C.T.** It all goes back to management weaknesses and preferences and predilections of artistic directors, many of whom lack a sense of balance in making judgments and decisions.

Still considering the comments which artists made earlier in this chapter, one wonders if it is significant, for example, that while one hundred and thirty years ago Edwin Booth established a reputa-tion for himself in the Bay area, it was necessary for him to go to New York to become a star of first magnitude and to make a respect-able living at his art, and that many of today's young actors still feel it is necessary to go to New York or Los Angeles to achieve real success. If so, what does this say about the progress of theatre in and around San Francisco? What does it say about opportunities for artists in this area?

Many of the people interviewed in this chapter responded in ways which made them sound disillusioned and disappointed. It should be remembered, though, that artists throughout history have experienced struggle, deprivation and frustration. The best of them have had their ups and downs, and perhaps the heartbreak of these interviewees is no more severe than that of artists of other areas. The strongest do survive.

The theatre, too, survives. Consider how Maguire's theatres were destroyed in the earthquakes of 1849-'51 and how he rebuilt them; consider how talking pictures nearly killed local theatres in the early 1930s and how the **Wayfarers** and other groups of the 40s and 50s rekindled the flames of live performances and somehow kept the traditions of San Francisco theatre going. Will the Reagan administration and the lessening distribution of funds by the **National Endowment for the Arts** kill our theatre? I can't be - lieve they will. Would an increased number of grants given to Bay area artists and theatres make local productions really better? Perhaps. Perhaps not.

Some of the people interviewed in this chapter will indeed leave San Francisco to seek their fortunes in New York or Holly - wood; some will find those fortunes and others will not. Isn't it meaningful, though, that a large number of the people quoted in these pages—whether they be actors, directors, playwrights or de - signers—are long-time residents of the area, despite the many work problems and frustrations which they have faced? That says something. I wouldn't be surprised, either, if most of them continue to live right here for the rest of their lives. Artists are basically opti - mists, you know. That's what makes them gallants.

Magic Theatre's *The Couch* featured (left to right) Kenna Hunt, Jack Shearer,
Molly Stadum, Gerald Winer and Francia di Mase, 1985. (Photo: Allen Nomura)

Asian-American Theatre Company's production of *Thirst* featured Sharon Iwai, Fay Kawabata and Nadja Kennedy, 1985. (above, Photo: AAT Collection)

Dennis Barnett, Sigrid Wurschmidt, Julian Lopez-Morillas and Jack Shearer in the Eureka production of *Gardenia*, 1986. (below, Photo: Allen Nomura)

The Julian Theatre scored a success with Marsha Norman's *Getting Out* with J. E. Freeman and Saun Ellis in 1980.
(Photo: Allen Nomura)

J. J. Johnson and Kitty Newman were leading players in Nova Theatre's *Sarah and the Sax*, 1986.
(Photo: Bill Hendrickson)

Kathleen McCormick, Mark Chaet, Cynthia Simmons and Anthony J. Haney performed in the Lorraine Hansberry Theatre's *A Raisin in the Sun*, 1984 (above; Photo: Allen No - mura). Director J. Kevin Hanlon confers with actor Daniel Osmon on the set of Theatre Rhinoceros's *The International Stud*, 1981. (below; Photo: Rink)

Arthur Miller's *Playing for Time* at the One Act Theatre in late 1985 featured the women in the above photo. (Photo: Marshall Berman)

Jaston Williams and Joe Sears headed the original San Francisco cast of *Greater Tuna*, 1984. (below; Photo: Ken Howard)

The Eureka Theatre's 1986 production of *The Cherry Orchard* featured Abigail Van Alyn and Brian Thompson. (above; Photo: Allen Nomura)

Ebbe Roe Smith, Carol McElheney and Jim Haynie (l. to r.) appeared in the Magic Theatre's production of Sam Shepard's *True West*, 1979-'80 (facing page, above; Photo: Allen Nomura). *The Homecoming*, a Chamber Theatre production featured (clockwise from top left) Michael Bellino, Michael Girardin, Abe Kalish, Dan O'Connor, Bernie Segal and Jennifer Grimes, 1986. (facing page, below; Photo: Ken Grimes)

William Paterson and Joan Stuart-Morris in A.C.T.'s *Opéra Comique*, 1985. (above; Photo: Larry Merkle)

Marrian Walters and Elizabeth Huddle in A.C.T.'s *'Night Mother*, 1986. (facing page, above; Photo: Larry Merkle)
Drew Eshelman, Dean Goodman, Peter Jacobs and Wendell J. Grayson form a group of conspirators in *The Passion Cycle*, A.C.T., 1986. (facing page, below; Photo: Larry Merkle)

Edward Hastings, General Director A.C.T. 1986. (Photo: Hank Kranzler)

10

FUTURE—TENSE!

Maxim Gorki once said the only thing which is constant is struggle. One can assume that the great Russian playwright was re ferring to his own work in the theatre when he made that observation. But he might also, if he had chosen to do so, have observed that while basic problems remain pretty much the same, in both the theatre and life itself, there can be changes in the way human beings deal with these problems.

Nearly everybody will agree that there is no shortage of talent in San Francisco theatre. Tony Taccone of the **Eureka** speaks positively of his theatre's future, the maturity of his company and its determination to create a body of original material which can "imagi natively express ideas that bear directly on our lives." Simon Levy, artistic director of the **One Act**, suggests that a certain disillusionment exists among theatre artists because "we have become more concerned with the business of theatre than with the art of what we're presenting." Levy recommends a re-examination of personal goals and an eventual determination of whether "we wish to be artists or institutions." Levy's observations, of course, are prompted by his concern over the economics of present-day theatre.

But economics have always been a problem, in the theatre as well as the other arts. The business of the theatre is a fact of life, whether one likes it or not. Much better to accept that fact and deal with it, rather than ignore it. The rent has to be paid, playwrights are entitled to royalties for their work, and the performers deserve recompense for their efforts. Nothing is gained by denying this.

In a sense, with many foundations and corporations supplying grants to them, San Francisco theatres have enjoyed privileges in recent years which companies of other times did not. In 1931, when the **Wayfarers** helped to keep theatre alive here, and later when the **Interplayers**, the **Playhouse**, the **Company of the Golden Hind** and the **Actor's Workshop** followed suit, there were no foundation grants to help such companies. (The **Workshop** re-ceived its first grant from the **Ford Foundation** in 1960.) These groups depended on survival solely from box-office receipts and from the generosity of occasional private benefactors. The **Eureka**, the **One Act**, the **Magic**, the **Julian** and **A.C.T.** have more re-sources for funds than their predecessors, even with recent cuts made in monies doled out by the **National Endowment for the Arts** (**NEA**) and other funding groups. In this regard, they might count a few blessings.

There has long been a debate over whether or not the arts should be subsidized in the United States as they are in other coun-tries. Regarding an announcement that the **National Endowment for the Arts** was making a tremendous cutback in grants be-stowed, Joseph Papp of the **New York Shakespeare Festival** was quoted in the July 2, 1981 issue of the *Hollywood Reporter* as saying that "the arts deserve no special privileges. I think the con-cept of beginning to appraise how money is spent is good for the arts and should be ongoing. We also have to develop a kind of wel-fare mentality and move our asses a little bit ourselves."

I happen to be in favor of government subsidy, and I think that corporations and foundations should be encouraged to make grants to San Francisco theatres. But I also think they should look more carefully into the way the money they donate is being spent, as Papp suggests. Some of the small theatre managers in San Francisco at the present time seem to feel that artistry and business acumen are incompatible, and that to develop a business sense means compro-mise of artistic standards. This is not really true. Many of history's greatest artists have also been keen business people. It is possible

140

for a theatre company to produce fine art and yet operate sensibly, with sound business practices, and if San Francisco is to grow and improve as a theatre town then the managements of the local companies must realize this. Otherwise, provincial "little theatre" attitudes can only prevail. With cutbacks in corporate funding, such companies as the **One Act**, the **Eureka** and the **Magic** may have to become more independent and, as Papp says, "move their asses" a little bit themselves if they are to survive.

In the preface to this volume I stated that one of the more controversial aspects of *San Francisco Stages* might be the things I have to say about the critics and about the kind of press coverage which the theatre community receives in San Francisco. I'm not going to go as far as David Mamet by declaring that any of the critics here are the syphilis or the gonorrhea of our theatre, but I do agree with Jane Fonda as quoted in the Sunday *Examiner-Chronicle* when she said,"I think we have a terrible press, just absolutely terrible" and I agree also with Richard Dreyfuss's comment, "When critics are jerks they deserve to be the object of my wrath," as quoted in Peter Stack's interview with the actor in the January 21, 1982 edition of the *Chronicle*. If press coverage of San Francisco theatre does not improve I truly fear for the kinds of standards which the public will be encouraged to develop. Readers are fed misinforma - tion and half-truths every day of their lives in the major publications.

When Bernard Weiner refers, as he did in the *Chronicle* of April 13, 1982 to "Noel Coward's 1939 comedy *Design for Living* " one can perhaps be tolerant and shrug off this blooper with an indulgent smile. Real theatre buffs will know what year Coward's play was first produced, and perhaps it doesn't matter that much if Weiner was a bit off the mark. On the other hand, when the drama editor of the leading newspaper in northern California refuses to re - tract statements (such as he made in March of 1982, asserting that **Equity** members in the Bay area were voting to eliminate the waiver and claiming that this move was a "New York plan") even when presented with documentary evidence of his error, the man is not just making a forgivable mistake; he is misleading his readers and misrecording history. When Barbara Shulgasser of the *Exam - iner* declares in a review that G. B. Shaw was not a good play - wright and that it took Lerner and Loewe to make *Pyg - malion* theatrically viable, and when a man named Randy Lyman tells us in the *Sentinel U.S.A.* that he "can't imagine what attrac -

tion" a play like Noel Coward's *Private Lives* holds for today's audiences and that the script for this classic comedy of manners is "leaden" we realize that, to put it mildly, some of our local critics are naive and inexperienced. Haven't we had enough, too, of the arro - gant smart-ass tone which pervades some of the reviews in the *Chronicle*, the *Examiner* and the gay give-away papers? What these writers may consider brilliant wit too often comes across in their re - views as childish and superficial evaluation. While I certainly agree with Misha Berson that **A.C.T.** "belongs to all of us to some degree" (as she stated in the March 12, 1986 *Bay Guardian*) and while I concede that she is as much entitled as anyone to make constructive suggestions, I shudder to think what the San Francisco theatre scene would be like if **A.C.T.** or the **Eureka** or the **Magic** or the **S. F. Repertory** or the **One Act** produced only the kinds of plays which she recommends in her article. One thing that is good about these companies is the difference in their philosophies. **A.C.T.** should not be turned into the **Mime Troupe**, nor vice versa. Different styles and philosophies *should* flourish in a healthy theatre community and decent critics should be sympathetic to such differences and encourage them. We must always have a place for new plays by Sam Shepard and his like, but we must also have a place for revivals of comic operas by Gilbert and Sullivan.

It saddens me to write so disparagingly of our San Francisco critics. I wish I could compliment them all on jobs well done. But my files are too full of their errors and discrepancies; I am too conscious of how they are misrecording history. One of my chief reasons for writing this book, in fact, is to speak out about this unhappy state of affairs and to advise readers that they must not accept everything they read in the pages of the *Chronicle* or the *Examiner* as absolute truth.

For the past thirty years the chief critics and drama reporters on the *Chronicle* and the *Examiner* have been people who have been transferred to the entertainment section from other pages of the pa - pers. Between the mid-50s and the mid-70s this situation wasn't too bad. Paine Knickerbocker, who took over the post on the *Chron - icle* in the mid-50s, had a lot to learn but at least he *knew* that he had a lot to learn. Because he was a gentleman, and a humble gentle - man, we could go along with him while he developed his skills. Stanley Eichelbaum, who took over the reins on the *Examiner* from Hortense Morton during the season of 1958-'59, made a reputation for himself over the years as temperamental and acerbic (he told me that he received a lot of hate mail and that an artist he had criticized spat in his face on one occasion) but at least Eichelbaum had innate good taste and a respect for professionalism. With a few exceptions, the present critics in San Francisco have only an academic knowl -edge of the theatre and, I'm afraid, they are living examples of the Peter Principle in action. Holding an administrative position, no matter how effectively, with the **Theatre Communications Cen -ter** or directing a Joe Orton play in a little theatre in Berkeley does not supply a man or woman with sufficient credentials to evaluate the work of artists who have spent a lifetime perfecting their crafts. It is the publishers who are to blame for employing such people.

Make no mistake about it, these kinds of people who are now in power with the press will heavily influence the San Francisco the -atre of the future. Theatre companies will choose to present plays which the critics prefer, or which they think the critics prefer, and they will be reluctant to hire directors or actors who are not praised and favored by the leading reviewers. (I suspect that one of the reasons, if not the major reason, that William Ball resigned from **A.C.T.** was that he was simply weary of continued attacks against him in the *Chronicle*, the *Examiner* and the *Bay Guardian*. It should be noted, however, that it was Knickerbocker and Eichelbaum who supported **A.C.T.** in the beginning; it is their *successors* who have done their best to destroy **A.C.T.**'s image in the public eye.) Yes, make no mistake about it, the personal tastes of the new critics will determine, to a great extent, not only what plays you and I will be permitted to see in San Francisco over the next few years but also which directors and which actors will be permitted to work.

Is there anything which can be done about it? Not much, I fear. Letters to the editor, objecting to a critic's position on a production or a performance, are seldom printed; when they are published they are frequently cut. No, there isn't much any of us can do to prevent the kind of idiocy which goes on. I never heard of a critic changing his position because of a letter of protest. The only suggestion I can make to those of you who read these pages is that you support the kind of theatre and the performers which *you* like, regardless of what Weiner, Winn, Shulgasser, Nachman, Berson or any of the others try to tell you.

While cognizant of the many problems which beset the San Francisco theatre scene, I don't wish to convey a negative outlook for its future. The struggle which Maxim Gorki wrote about may be constant among actors, playwrights, directors, administrators and even critics, but changes can be made and improvements are desirable. Following here is a list of a few goals which I would like to see reached before the end of this century.

1) I hope that, as soon as possible, editors and publishers will begin to recruit more qualified people to work as reviewers and reporters. By qualified people I mean people who have had some practical professional experience in the theatre and have enjoyed some success in it. (Is there a person alive who loves the theatre and is over ten years old who hasn't seen *A Chorus Line*? Well, believe it or not, the *Examiner* sent a reviewer to cover the umpteenth road company of this show at the **Golden Gate Theatre** who con - fessed in her review of March 28, 1986 that she had never seen this classic musical. Now I can accept the fact that a theatre-wise person might not have seen *Pump Boys and Dinette* or even *Zorba* before, but *A Chorus Line*? Come on! Sudden thought: do you suppose the *Examiner* reviewer really *isn't* over ten years old?) Qualified crit - ics, people with good backgrounds, don't necessarily have to be "names" or Broadway or Hollywood stars of any kind, but they should have more than just an academic knowledge of what they're writing about; they should understand the creative process in an organic way, and this can only be accomplished through the experience of it. Yes, I'm well aware that many of the current editors and critics will disagree with me on this point; that's because they haven't got the experience I'm talking about and they are natur - ally placed on the defensive. But I put fair and knowledgeable press coverage at the top of my priority list for improvements needed in San Francisco theatre, because the press has such a profound influ - ence on the quality and success of local productions. A former sports writer or society editor, or a layman who has taken a couple of drama courses in college, is not equipped to evaluate art nor qualified to tell the public at large what is good and what isn't, what should be supported and what shouldn't. It is the editors and pub - lishers, mainly, who must steer the theatre in the right direction by choosing the best people available to write for them. "Just anybody" who applies when the job opening is announced won't do the work well. The bosses must *seek out* the best people.

2) I urge the current critics, many of whom will be around for a while, to adopt a little humility and recognize, as Paine Knicker -

144

bocker did, that they have a few things to learn themselves. I urge them to take a long, hard look at their criteria for evaluating a play or production and also to clean up their practices and policies in report - ing the theatre news. A play or an actor's performance should be judged for its believability, its style, its mood and many technical aspects, but most important is its overall intent. Whether or not that intent is compatible with what the critic personally likes is irrelevant when considering whether or not the artist has done commendable work. In judging actors, the performer's versatility should be con - sidered in evaluating his general skill and talent. Is the actor, for example, as adept at playing Molière as he is at interpreting one of David Mamet's street characters? To determine this, of course, the study of a body of work is required. I hope, therefore, that the San Francisco critics will be a little more cautious about declaring an absolute novice some sort of genius, when nine times out of ten he's never heard from again, while at the same time damning with faint praise or totally ignoring artists who have done consistently good work over a long period of time. (Steven Winn, in his *Chron - icle* review of a **Magic Theatre** play on March 29, 1986 called the work of a totally unknown actor "superb"; two days earlier, in his review of **A.C.T.**'s *The Passion Cycle* he couldn't bring himself to give more than perfunctory acknowledgment to several actors who have given the Bay area fine performances for years.)

If dramatic criticism is to have any valid purpose, apart from merely advising the public what to see or what not to see, it should be a thoughtful analysis of a production or performance with sug - gestions as to how it might have been improved. (Barbara Shulgas - ser did almost the same as Winn in her *Examiner* review of *The Passion Cycle*. She conceded that four actors had mastered the recitation of verse, as if that were the only thing required of them, but gave the major space in her review to derogatory similes describing the actor who essayed the role of Jesus. What these two critics reveal about themselves, therefore, is that they relish snub - bing or degrading actors—at least actors who are not among their personal favorites—more than they enjoy finding something for which to credit them.) Negative criticism accomplishes no good whatsoever, not even for the critic who writes it. I hope that the current critics will stop practicing their personal vendettas and stop giving vent to their own frustrations and hostilities in the public press.

145

I hope, too, that these critics will learn to be more accurate in reporting the news. One theatre administrator told me he wouldn't talk to the press at all anymore, because too often (under the guise of expressing varied opinions) reporters solicit quotes from sources which are totally uninformed, then give these views equal credence in print with statements made by the people who are truly knowl - edgeable. The well-informed source can therefore be discredited, if it suits the whim of the reporter. At other times a theatre reporter will get a kernel of the truth and interpret it in such a way that a total misrepresentation of the event or issue is conveyed to the public. (Judith Green, a theatre writer for the San Jose *Mercury News*, for example, reported that William Ball announced his resignation from **A.C.T.** on the set of *The Passion Cycle* standing before the cross, thus implying a symbolic significance to the occasion. I was there; I saw and heard what happened. Ball did announce his resignation following a rehearsal of the crucifixion scene, but he did not stand in front of the cross nor anywhere near it. Green's story distorted what actually occurred and made it appear as if the director had staged some sort of calculated melodramatic event. An erroneous impres - sion was therefore conveyed to the reading public.) I do hope that theatre reporters will be more careful in selecting their sources and screening their facts in the future.

Just as I complete this text and hand it over to my publishers, Bernard Weiner has announced in the *Chronicle* (April 5, 1986) that there will be a gathering of theatre critics and reviewers this summer in conjunction with the **Bay Area Playwrights Festival**. Orga - nized by Misha Berson, the three day event "will give both seasoned and novice theatre critics a chance to share knowledge, learn from visiting master critics, examine the ethics of criticism and exchange views on local theatre." While one wonders just who the "seasoned" and "master" critics could possibly be, the thought occurs that such a seminar could be very useful and productive if handled in the right way. Instead of inviting a group of critics and reporters merely to exchange views with each other, however (which might be pretty much a case of the blind leading the blind), I suggest that the critics would learn far more about the theatre and the ethics of criticism if Berson were to invite a cross section of actors, directors and play - wrights to meet with them for their discussions. I guarantee they'd get an earful. Of course, such a procedure would be revolutionary since, as we all know, critics are fully entitled to destroy any artist they wish in their reviews but they, being blessed with divinity, are above any kind of criticism themselves. Nevertheless, sessions with experienced working artists could teach these people far more than any lessons they might learn from mutual back-patting.

3) San Francisco theatre will be much improved in all respects when administrators and artistic directors recognize the importance of good business acumen. Happily, the San Francisco Experiment which **Equity** actors forced on the local managers in 1982 has re - sulted in better organization, stricter discipline in work habits, better pay for all theatre artists, and a greater respect for human rights. There are still some administrators who are resentful of this develop - ment, however, resistant to their own growth, and paranoid about **Equity**'s attempts to help them become more professional. They still equate chaotic operation with artistic integrity; they still cling to the provincial "little theatre" way of doing things. Perhaps there will always be a few administrators and a few companies on the local scene which retain an amateur status, and perhaps there's nothing wrong with that. Perhaps San Francisco theatre will never be as to - tally professional as New York theatre, or Chicago theatre, but it certainly ought to be as professional as Seattle theatre. At the present time it isn't. Yes, even Seattle employs more **Equity** actors than San Francisco on a regular basis. This situation won't change until enough San Francisco managers recognize that while sometimes fine art can be produced under impossible conditions this does not have to be the rule. Good work can be done under good conditions, too. I think the signs for San Francisco theatre along these lines are en - couraging. More and more producers are accepting the fact that if they want to produce good shows in San Francisco they must work under the conditions which **Equity** recommends, and more and more of them are doing it. Bay area **Equity** actors can take a lot of credit for spurring this development. It bodes well for the future.

4) I would like to see even more diversity in the kinds of plays which are produced in San Francisco, both independently and by the established companies. Theatrical happenings and performance art works with unusual audio and visual effects are fine; there's a growing audience for this kind of thing. But let us not conclude that everything produced must be unconventional in form to be worth doing. The **Magic Theatre** had one of its greatest successes with *The Couch*, a play which was not at all abstract but quite realistic in form and content. There may be a lesson in that success, in the

enthusiasm with which even the **Magic** audience responded. I applaud the **Eureka** for presenting Chekhov's *The Cherry Orchard* , albeit Trevor Griffith's "modern" adaptation of the classic in the spring of 1986; a theatre company can only grow and improve if it extends itself beyond the borders by which it won its original ac‑ claim. We do not, however, need a rock 'n' roll version of *King Lear* or a futuristic *Star Wars*-like interpretation of *Romeo and Juliet* to make us appreciate the majesty of Shakespeare's themes and the beauty of his language. I think we've had enough of this kind of game-playing. We will, however, always welcome good new plays. But, since the American theatre has built a library of its own classics over the past sixty years, shouldn't some of our theatres (other than **A.C.T.**) present us occasionally with a first-rate revival? I can think of a dozen plays from the 30s and 40s, for example, which deal with themes as relevant today as when they were first produced. Audiences of the 80s might find much to ad‑ mire in these plays, and the theatres might broaden their subscription bases if they were to include an occasional drama by Sidney Howard or Elmer Rice, or an early comedy by Kaufman and Hart.

5) Much good would be accomplished, I think, if artistic di‑ rectors and stage directors would change their approach to casting. The prepared-piece audition is not the only way to cast a play, and it may not be the best way, either. But many directors seem hemmed in by this process (which is relatively new in the theatre, inci‑ dentally). Some directors in San Francisco, when starting to cast a play, think immediately of personal friends or lovers for the avail‑ able parts. (This isn't necessarily a bad thing; some of the friends and lovers may be good actors and comfortable working partners.) On the other hand, it is foolhardy to depend on the right actors for particular roles to show up for open auditions. Many good actors don't go to cattle calls. Established actors in New York or Holly‑ wood never go to open auditions; they are contacted through agents and asked to read from the script, perhaps, or simply offered parts because the director or producer is familiar with their work. There is no reason why a similar process couldn't be followed in San Francisco. True, we don't have agents in the Bay area who work for actors as they do in Hollywood and New York. But directors could see actors as they perform with other theatre companies; not nearly enough of our **Eureka**, **Magic** and **One Act** directors attend other theatres regularly, and they should, to get an idea of the wealth of

talent we have here and the versatility of local performers. As I've recommended that publishers seek out the best people to work as critics, I also recommend that directors seek out the most skilled and experienced actors for roles in their plays. They can only do this if they make an effort on their own. I hope they will do this more and more in the future.

When the publishers of the major press institute better hiring policies, when critics and reviewers are better educated, when the - atre managers adopt better business tactics, when artistic directors choose a diversity of plays to produce, and when stage directors seek out the best and most experienced actors to appear in their pro - ductions we can look forward to a much more healthy and thriving theatre community in the Bay area. The state I describe here is an ideal, of course, but it is not an impossible state to achieve.

On publication of John Wilk's book *The Creation of an En - semble* Nancy Scott interviewed the author for the *Examiner.* The tone of Scott's interview implied that she was displeased because Wilk seemed to write favorably of **A.C.T.**, as if this were some sort of mark against him. It has indeed been the fashion of late to trash **A.C.T.** in the press, and I expect I, like John Wilk, will be accused of favoritism and "slanting" my material in this volume because I have refused to join the hatchet crowd. The fact is, I am as aware as anyone of mistakes which have been made at **A.C.T.** but I am also aware that there has never been a more prestigious theatre company in San Francisco since the first recorded performance in Portsmouth Square in 1849. I believe that much needs to be said at this time in **A.C.T.**'s defense. Despite its detractors, **A.C.T.** has been for twenty years and remains today the flagship theatre in the Bay area theatre community.

With William Ball's resignation and Edward Hastings' ap - pointment as the company's new general director **A.C.T.** enters a new era. Ball leaves to work in films and television and Hastings, who has worked closely with Ball since the company first came to San Francisco, takes over the helm. Because of the close association which these two men have had over the past twenty years, Hastings' appointment assures all concerned that there will be some continuity in company policies. Everything which **A.C.T.** has stood for over the past twenty years will not go down the drain. Hastings is his own man, however, and changes here and there are sure to occur.

I met with Ed Hastings in early April, 1986, shortly after the announcement of his assignment. He was pleased and excited about his new duties. "Ever since I started out in the theatre," he said, "I've wanted to be a producer with my own company."

Hastings is on record as approving the idea of an ensemble acting company. "But since it was announced that I was to be **A.C.T.**'s new general director, the number of letters and phone calls I've received has reminded me that the **A.C.T.** family isn't just forty actors. It's more like four hundred, and many of them are willing to come back home for a play now and then." He remarked how well Fredi Olster and Rick Hamilton, who were key actors with the company in the mid-70s, fitted back into the groove when they returned to play *Private Lives* and *The Lady's Not for Burning* in the spring of 1986. "It was as if they'd never been away," he said. Hastings mentioned no specific names, but he did intimate that he expected other "old-timers" to return to the fold. (At press time Ruth Kobart was reported to be cast in *Sunday in the Park with George* opening in October, 1986.)

"However," he went on, "some of these actors are now making bigger money, and they can't commit themselves for a full season of rep at the money we can afford to pay. So there may have to be some modification of the rotating rep idea. There are advantages and disadvantages to be considered. Maybe we'll have rotating rep two or three months out of the season and regular runs at the opening and at the end. I don't know yet."

At the time we talked Hastings was not ready to announce the schedule of plays for the 1986-'87 season, but he indicated that some sort of announcement would have to be made by the first of June. "That's when we'll start our new subscription drive." He wants to include some plays on the schedule which have special meaning to the community. (Editor's note: *Following the author's completion of his text, and as this book goes to press, Edward Hastings has announced* **Sunday in the Park with George, The Doctor's Dilemma, The Seagull, The Real Thing, The Floating Light Bulb, Ma Rainey's Black Bottom** *and* **Faustus in Hell** *as A.C.T's schedule of plays for the 1986-'87 season.*)

It was Hastings who instituted the Plays-In-Progress series at **A.C.T.** He also fostered the group which eventually became the **Asian-American Theatre**. There is good reason to believe he will not only encourage the development of new plays within the company, but will perhaps come up with other innovative ideas to stimulate public interest. On the day we met, the new director had just come from a meeting of the trustees and fundraisers. He was pleased that the noted octogenarian Cyril Magnin, former president of the **California Association for A.C.T.** but inactive on the company's behalf for the past five years, had been made an honorary member of the new board of directors. An annual free matinee for school children will be presented in Magnin's name.

With Edward Hastings taking over as the new head of **A.C.T.**, aided by actor/director Joy Carlin who has returned to the company, and with many of the smaller theatres moving to full professional contracts, it seems clear that San Francisco theatre has entered a promising period in the middle 80s. The constant struggle to which Maxim Gorki referred will continue, of course. Absolute perfection can never be achieved. Artists find their dignity, however, like Sisyphus in the ancient myth, ever striving for the top of the mountain, falling back a few paces now and then but forging ahead with spirit and determination and hope for a better future. It is the radical expression of that hope which enables us to continue to live in this world.

Dean Goodman as Hamlet, on tour throughout Can -
ada in 1953. (above; Photo: Eric Skipsey)

Meryl Shaw (below, right) chairperson of SF/BAAC
presents Dean Goodman with a plaque in recognition
of his years of service to Actors' Equity, March,
1986. (Photo: Harry Rosenbluth)

"It may be," wrote critic Paine Knickerbocker in the San Francisco Chronicle on February 8, 1974, "that Dean Goodman has had a greater variety of theatrical roles and responsibilities than any other individual connected with the stage in the Bay area."

Goodman's extensive experience has indeed given him a unique overview of San Francisco theatre, both as an art and as a business. He has produced, directed or acted in close to four hundred plays during his lifetime. His reviews and feature articles have appeared in the Seattle Argus, the Hollywood Citizen-News and Hol - lywood Drama-Logue, among others. He served two terms as president of the Bay Area Theatre Critics Circle and two terms as president of the San Francisco Council On Entertainment. Recipient of several nominations and awards for his acting performances, he was recently presented with a plaque by Actors Equity in recognition of his years of service to the union. In fact, as writer Jori Parr put it in her Chronicle article of August 5, 1979, "It is tempting to call [Dean Goodman] the dean of San Francisco theatre."

Following four years (1938-'42) as leading juvenile with the original Seattle Repertory, he became a protégé of the famed Russian actress Maria Ouspenskaya in Hollywood, where he acted on many of the prominent NBC-CBS radio shows of the period and appeared in plays at the Pasadena Playhouse. Later in New York he managed four summer theatres, including the renowned Provincetown Playhouse, produced a road company of *O Mistress Mine!* starring Sylvia Sidney, John Loder and Dick Van Patten, and acted with Jose Ferrer, Jane Cowl and Arlene Francis.

In 1952, following two seasons as director and leading man with the Cirque Playhouse in Seattle, Goodman was invited to play Macbeth with the Everyman Repertory Company in Vancouver, B.C. He remained with this company to direct and act in other productions, and his Hamlet, on tour throughout Canada in 1953, was labelled superb and a work of consummate art by leading critics.

Dean Goodman's first appearance in San Francisco was at the Geary Theatre in 1943, while on tour with John Carradine in Shakespearean repertory. He came back to teach drama at San Francisco State University in 1955. Since that time he has appeared as an actor with dozens of theatre companies in this vicinity, including the noted Actor's Workshop. His most recent appearances, as this book goes to press, were with the American Conservatory Theatre, where he played Crampton in Shaw's *You Never Can Tell* and Pontius Pilate in *The Passion Cycle* in the spring of 1986. His many directing credits include *Tartuffe* with Victor Buono, *Candida* with Sylvia Sidney, *The Merchant of Venice* with John Carradine, *Othello* with Brock Peters, and *The Late Christopher Bean* with Zasu Pitts. No stranger to musical comedy, Dean Goodman has played Merlin in *Camelot* with Pernell Roberts, the Starkeeper in *Carousel* with Robert Goulet, Leslie Uggams' father in *The Boy Friend* and Pearl Bailey's secretary in *Call Me Madam.*

Divorced from Maria Seiber, daughter of German film director Rudolph Seiber and actress Marlene Dietrich, in 1946, Goodman has never remarried. "But I'm far from lonely," he says. "I have good friends, an active social life, and there are always projects on the fire. My health is excellent and I've never had a serious accident. God has been good to me. I've done a little bit of everything I've ever wanted to do, and I'm grateful for that. Life is still a tremendous adventure."

INDEX

154

155

157

159

Index

Los Gatos 31
Lotta's Fountain 6
Louise M. Davies Symphony Hall.
  See Davies Symphony Hall
Love Watches 15
Lovis, David 92
Lowell High School 25, 26
Low Moan Spectacular Company 74
Lunchtime Theatre 58
Lunt, Alfred 21, 22, 25
Lunts, The 21-23, 25, 30
Lyman, Randy 141
Lynch, Michael 58
McCadden, Wanda 59
McCallum, David 78
McClure, Michael 57, 105
McCommons, Warren R. 92
MacDonald, Donald 20
Mace, Harriet 3
McIntyre and Heath 18
McNight, Sharon 104
Madame Sarah 14
Mad Booths of Maryland, The 2
Made in Heaven 13
Madwoman of Chaillot, The 32
Magic Theatre 33, 56-58, 102-107,
  118, 136, 137, 140-142, 145, 147,
  148
Magnin, Cyril 151
Maguire, Thomas 2-4, 6, 137
Maguire's Minstrels 6
Maids, The 34, 106
Make Room for Daddy 36
Mame 90
Mamet, David 95, 141
Manley, Beatrice 37
Mann, Winifred 39
Manners, Hartley 18
Mantell, Robert 16
Man with the Golden Arm, The 34
Ma Rainey's Black Bottom 150
Marchetti, Will 34, 57
March of the Falsettos 62
Marco Polo 79
Margaret and Ernie versus the
  World 58
Margaret Jenkins Dance Studio 56

Marina Junior High School 31
Marin County 35, 56, 66
Marines Memorial Theatre 25, 37, 40,
  42, 56, 57, 65, 77, 78, 127
Marsden, Susan 56, 102
Martin, Ernest. *See* Feuer and Martin
Martin, Mary 25, 26
Mary Stuart 9
Mason, Marsha 41, 106
Mason, Mary 56
Mason Street Theatre 77, 81
Mass Appeal 71
Massett, Stephen 1, 2
Master Builder, The 34
Matchmaker, The 24, 32
Matter of Gravity, A 26
Matthews, Dakin 41, 51
Maugham, William Somerset 14
Maxine Elliott Theatre 13, 14
Max Reinhardt Studio 27
Melodyland 14
Melville, Emilie 20, 21
Memory of Two Mondays, A 32
Merchant of Venice, The 26
Mercury News 152
Mercutio 23
Merman, Ethel 25
Merriam, Eve 71
Merrick, David 24
Merrill, Gary 25
Merry Widow, The 85
Metropolitan Theatre 4, 5
Meyer, Arthur 35
Michelle 91
Micro Pro Litera Press iv
Midgie Purvis 24
Midsummer Night's Dream, A 8, 9
Mikado, The 18
Miksak, Joseph 39, 57, 59
Miller, Arthur 16, 32, 37, 58
Miller, Norma 34
Mills College 32
Mime Troupe 36, 67, 86, 87, 106,
  142
Miranda, Carmen 84
Miss Innocence 17
Mission Dolores 2

166

Stowe, Harriet Beecher 8
Strange Bedfellows 31
Strange Interlude 23
Streep, Meryl 100
Strindberg, August 34
Studio Eremos 62
Subsidiary Rights Agreement
  (SRA) 48-50
Sullivan, Sir Arthur. *See* Gilbert and
  Sullivan
Summer Training Congress 42
Sunday in the Park with George 150
Sweeney Todd 47, 97
Sylvester the Cat vs. Galloping Billy
  Bronco 58
Symonds, Robert 38
Synge, John M. 92
Taccone, Anthony 56, 139
Tale Spinners 59, 62, 92, 93
Talley's Folly 71
Taming of the Shrew, The 4, 22, 78
Tandy, Jessica 25
Tartuffe 40, 41
Taylor, Charles 18
Taylor, Laurette 18, 19
TCCBA. *See* Theatre Communi -
  cations Center of the Bay Area
Tea and Sympathy 34
Telegraph Hill 3
Telfer, Ronald 30
Terry, Ellen 8
Tetrazzini, Luisa 17
Theatre Artaud 62
Theatre Arts Colony 34
Theatre Arts Magazine 31, 34
Theatre Communications Center of the
  Bay Area (TCCBA) 88, 127, 143
Theatre Guild 25
Theatre Guild of San Francisco 67
Theatre of the Absurd 33
Theatre-On-The-Square 64, 65, 71, 76,
  100
Theatre Rhinoceros 60, 67, 91, 118
Theatre Unlimited 92
There Was a Little Girl 79
They're Playing Our Song 75
Thomas, Danny 36

Thompson, Alice 89
Thou Swell 81
Three Sisters, The 43
Tierney, Ron 91
Tillie's Nightmare 17
Times (San Mateo) 99
Tiny Alice 41, 123
Tivoli Opera Association 20
Tivoli Opera Company 17
Tobacco Road 67
Todd, Mark 59
Tom Taylor as Woody Guthrie 71
Tonight at 8:30 13
Top Girl 56
Torch Song Trilogy 71, 76
Tour de Force 109
Trantham, Doug 79
Travers, Reginald 21, 30
Traviata, La 20
Trial of James McNeill Whistler,
  The 35
Trinity Episcopal Church 90
Trinity Methodist Church 55, 56
Tripp, Peter 58, 107
True West 57, 118
Truffaut, Michelle 59, 62, 90
Tubstrip 76
Tune the Grand Up 81
Twain, Mark 33
Twelfth Night 9
Twelve Pound Look, The 17
Twentieth-Century Fox 18, 27
2001 24
Uggams, Leslie 14
Ullery, Kirk 61
Ullman, Liv 95
Umbrellas of Cherbourg 45
Under the Yum-Yum Tree 14
University of California at Davis 73
Upton, Morgan 57
Valencia Rose 62
Valencia Theatre 15
Van Alyn, Abigail 57
Van Ness Theatre 15, 16
Vega, Ken 79
Venture Theatre 118
Verdier mansion 32, 33

168